Secrets of Effective Leadership

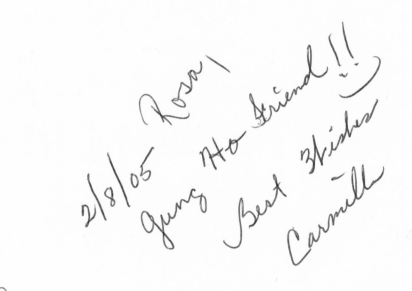

Rosa!
2/8/05 Gung Ho Friend !!
Best Wishes
Carmille

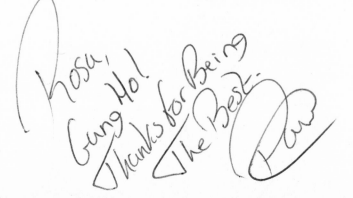

Rosa,
Gung Ho!
Thanks for Being
The Best.

Secrets of Effective Leadership

A Practical Guide to Success

Fred A. Manske, Jr.

**LEADERSHIP EDUCATION AND DEVELOPMENT, INC.
MOUNT PLEASANT, TN.**

2000 EDITION

Published by Leadership Education and Development, Inc.
113 First Avenue
Mount Pleasant, TN 38474
1-800-659-6135   www.leadershipdevelopment.com

Although the author and publisher have exhaustively researched all sources to ensure the accuracy and completeness of the information contained in this book, we assume no responsibility for errors, inaccuracies, omissions, or any inconsistency herein. All slights of people or organizations are unintentional.

First Edition, 1987
Second Edition, 1990
Third Edition, 1999
Fourth Edition, 2000

Printed in the United States of America.

Library of Congress Cataloging-in-Publication Data

Manske, Fred A., 1939-
    Secrets of effective leadership / Fred A. Manske, Jr. — 4th ed.

    Includes bibliographical references and index.
    ISBN 0943703-05-0: $15.95
    1. Leadership.   2. Executive ability.   I. Title.
HD57.7.M37   1999   98-89401
658.4'09—dc20

Contents

Acknowledgments

People develop their leadership skills by observing and emulating competent leaders and by being coached.

Over the years I have been fortunate to work for a number of outstanding leaders. Each person in a unique way contributed to the development of my leadership style. At Sealtest Foods, Bill Wade, Martin Downs, and Duane Malm coached me through my early years in management. Most of my middle-management career was spent at Eastern Airlines where I developed line and staff skills under the direction of George Bowers, Rick Rivenbank, Bob Walcott, and, most of all, Frank Borman.

For thirteen years I was associated with the unique company Federal Express and its chief operating officers Art Bass, Pete Willmott, Jim Barksdale and its innovative leader Fred Smith.

To all these gentlemen I express my deepest gratitude for the time and interest they invested in me.

There are two other significant people in my life that have been instrumental in shaping my leadership skills. They are my father, Fred A. Manske, Sr., and my father-in-law, Donald C. Harrison. In different but important ways each of them set examples of leadership worth emulating.

Finally, numerous individuals assisted me in the project of writing *Secrets of Effective Leadership.* Dr. George Jensen, Robert McEmber, Barbara Bekis, and Jeanne Thurman Cross assisted in the editing. Joy Walker Rhodes was instrumental in coordinating the printing and publication activities. And most of all, I thank my family (Donna and the children, Fred III, Don, and Cindy) whose love and understanding have given me strength to continually focus on my career. Together, they have provided a supportive, happy home where we have shared the experiences of the corporate life. Without them, the book would never have been possible.

Preface

Secrets of Effective Leadership: A Practical Guide to Success had its inception in the early 1970s when Mr. Manske worked for Eastern Airlines as Director of Training. He noticed that the management trainees were thirsty to learn from the experiences of respected leaders who made classroom presentations. The trainees were particularly interested in the stories of the leaders' past victories and failures. This led Mr. Manske to begin recording his own leadership experiences. Over the years he collected numerous anecdotes and inspirational quotations from outstanding leaders, past and present, from all walks of life.

Secrets of Effective Leadership sets the example for the highest standards of honesty and integrity in leaders at a time when such attributes are desperately needed in organizations. Several studies revealed a startling fact: A majority of employees working in large companies believe that management often lies and cheats.[1] With such widespread lack of trust, it is no wonder that people long to work for ethical, principled leaders who put the needs of the organization above their own.

The philosophy of the author is that people should be treated fairly and with dignity, not for what it will gain the leader, but because it is the right and decent thing to do.

Secrets of Effective Leadership is written from the perspective of someone who has been there in the trenches—at the front lines of the operating functions of business. Mr. Manske knows what it is like to work under constant pressure to improve quality, sales, and profits at higher and higher levels each year. He has worked with strong international unions and appreciates the difficulties of trying to lead employee groups during periods of rapid growth and severe economic downturns. This extensive hands-on experience helped the author identify and describe the secrets of leadership necessary for success in today's challenging business world.

The quick reference format is a unique aspect of the book. The chapters are designed to stand on their own. Readers can use *Secrets of Effective Leadership* as a **handbook** for guidance to solve leadership problems when they occur.*

Secrets of Effective Leadership emphasizes **practical** leadership principles and strategies that can be applied daily to inspire and energize people in organizations. Valuable ideas are presented on how to unleash your full leadership potential by (1) building on your leadership strengths and (2) managing both stress and your personal life.

Thoughtful study and application of the philosophies, principles, and ideas in *Secrets of Effective Leadership* **can be your guide to success!**

* *Since the publication of the first edition of this book, the Publisher has received numerous complimentary letters describing how it helped individuals in all walks of life to become better leaders. One interesting insight that was obtained from the feedback was that* **Secrets of Effective Leadership** *has relevance each time it is referred to or reread. This is because the conditions and situations faced by leaders are constantly changing, whereas the principles and philosophies of caring, ethical leadership are enduring.*

Introduction

There is a growing respect for leadership wisdom and experience in the corporate world. While management techniques, systems, and programs were revered a few years ago, a premium is now placed on leadership—obtaining excellence from people. For years, management placed insufficient attention on developing employees and inspiring them to be fully productive.

The trend toward increased emphasis on leadership is a reaction to the massive change that is occurring in the way business is conducted worldwide. The United States and Canada were once self-sufficient national economies. Now they are part of an interdependent global economy that features real-time information systems, just-in-time inventory replenishment, and time-based competition. The only way to successfully compete in such an economic environment is to produce high quality products and services at low cost.

This goal requires both sophisticated technology and the total dedication of employees to excellence—100 percent defect-free or error-free work. Excellence in an organization does not occur spontaneously. It is inspired, nurtured, and sustained by competent, ethical leaders.

Secrets of Effective Leadership was written with one purpose in mind: to contribute to the development of business leaders in today's technology driven, global economy by providing **practical** advice on how to obtain excellence from people.

Note: Throughout the book I've used the masculine and feminine genders interchangeably. Therefore, when I say "he" or "she" I am referring to both.

Ideals are like stars. You will not succeed in touching them with your hands. But like the seafaring man on the desert of waters, you choose them as your guides, and following them, you will reach your destiny.

Carl Schurz

I

What Is Leadership?

The art of leadership can be defined in many ways. Most definitions focus on the leader's role of inspiring others to achieve outstanding results.

Field Marshall Montgomery: "Leadership is the capacity and the will to rally men and women to a common purpose and the character which inspires confidence."

Vince Lombardi: "Coaches who can outline plays on the blackboard are a dime a dozen. The ones who succeed are those who can get inside their players and motivate them."

Peter Senge defines leadership in broader terms. He says: "It's about helping people make sense of what's going on around them and making people feel that complicated and challenging things can actually be done."

To me, a leader is a visionary who energizes others. This definition of leadership has two key dimensions: (a) creating a vision of the future and (b) inspiring people to make the vision reality.

Outstanding leaders are future oriented. They love to dream about what could be and to involve others in their dreams.

When a corporate leader has vision, he or she has an image or idea of what his or her organization should do in the future and how it should get there. In her classic management book *Dynamic Administration,* Mary Parker Follett commented on this vital aspect of leadership by saying, "The most successful leader of all is the one who sees another picture not actualized."[1]

Fredrick W. Smith had such a vision in the early 1970s. In a term paper for an economics course at Yale University he explained his vision of an air express system that would provide overnight and nationwide delivery of urgent packages. At the time, that vision seemed impractical and farfetched. In fact, Smith's economics professor gave him a "C" on the term paper. Undaunted, Smith used the ideas formulated in that "C" paper to create an A+ company—Federal Express. Today it is the world's largest air express and air freight carrier and is considered one of the best places to work in America.[2]

Another business leader who envisioned a product that significantly impacted America was Allen H. Neuharth, former chairman of the Gannet Corporation, a major publishing firm. His vision was that of a national newspaper delivered to homes and newsstands early each morning. Neuharth's dream was not to produce a traditional daily paper. He believed there was a whole new generation of readers who wanted the news presented in concise format utilizing colorful charts and graphs to explain world and national news, lifestyles, sports, and business.

Those that create, lead!

When the first edition of *USA Today* reached the streets on September 15, 1982, many people doubted it would succeed. As the annual losses grew, it appeared that the skeptics were right. Yet, Neuharth refused to abandon his dream of a unique newspaper. Finally, in late 1987, *USA Today* became profitable and obtained the largest daily circulation in America.

Martin Luther King, Jr., who led the great crusade for civil rights from 1955 to 1968, epitomized a leader with great vision and the tenacity to move ahead at all costs. Despite being jailed several times, stabbed, and stoned, King persisted in his efforts to fulfill his dream of a world of racial equality and improved living conditions for the poor.

Like small creeks that grow into mighty rivers, the dreams of leaders eventually shape the course of history.

No one, who was at the Washington Monument the afternoon of August 28, 1963, will ever forget the conclusion of King's speech before a crowd estimated to be over 250,000. Biographer Lerone Bennett, Jr., captured the electricity and emotion of the moment:

Digging deep within himself, picking up bits and pieces of speeches dating back to 1956, he began to improvise, rolling out long legato phrases that brought cheers like thunderous waves . . . over and over again King repeated, "I have a dream . . ." and the throng, electrified, rose en masse, screaming, cheering and crying, pushing him to ascending heights of revelations and discovery.[3]

Vision is therefore the first critical dimension of effective leadership. Without vision there is little hope or sense of purpose in an organization. Efforts drift aimlessly. The loss of purpose leads to a lack of coordination between work units and divisive infighting among managers.

If you don't know where you're going, you'll end up somewhere else.
Yogi Berra

Visions and intellectual strategies alone are insufficient to motivate and energize people at work. Sustained results come only if team members buy into a vision; they must believe that the leader's vision is **their** vision. Only then will they accept responsibility for achieving it. Herein lies the second key dimension of leadership: inspiring or energizing people to perform at their best individually and collectively.

It is not an easy task to get people to perform beyond what they think possible, to routinely give an extra 10 to 20 percent. Nor is it a simple procedure to mold a group of diverse individuals into a tight-knit team dedicated to excellence. Accomplishing both of these missions is the ultimate challenge of leadership and the primary focus of this book.

Outstanding leaders appeal to the hearts of their followers—not their minds.

John Naisbitt terms the energization of people to strive for a single vision "alignment."[4] In its highest form alignment exists when groups or teams of employees are totally dedicated to accomplishing the mission at hand and collaborate together unselfishly toward that end. At this point the goals of the organization and the individual are meshed or congruent.

The many ways that leaders energize others will be discussed in the following chapters. In general, however, **leaders create a positive attitude or force in their organizations.** They do this through the strength of their character and vision and by the creation of the feeling that good things are possible. Once this positive force begins, others in the group are stirred to action; soon an avalanche of enthusiasm is underway. Leadership in this sense provides hope and meaning for employees; the employees begin to believe that their own future goals can be realized through the organization's goals.

One of the greatest gifts we can give others is hope.

So far, leadership has been defined in terms of its two key dimensions: a vision of the company's purpose and the energization of people to achieve that purpose. Further understanding is available by comparing the information on leadership and management in the following table.

COMPARISON OF LEADERS AND MANAGERS

Leaders Tend to . . .	Managers Tend to . . .
Stress relationships with others, values and commitment—the emotional and spiritual aspects of the organization.	Stress organization, coordination, and control of resources (e.g., plant, equipment, and people).
Create and articulate a vision of what the organization could achieve in the long run.	Focus on the achievement of short-term objectives and goals.
Move the organization in new directions—being unsatisfied with maintaining the status quo.	Concentrate on maximizing results from existing functions and systems.
Empower people to act on their own to achieve objectives.	Insist that people check with him/her on every detail before they act.
Favor taking risks and making changes.	Fear uncertainty and act cautiously.
Generate a feeling of meaning in work—its value and importance.	Enforce fulfillment of agreements and contracts for work.
Frequently think strategically.	Seldom think strategically.
Have an insatiable passion to continuously develop themselves—eager to learn.	Tend not to push themselves to learn new things.

EFFECTIVE LEADERSHIP

Every organization needs both leaders and managers. **Leaders are needed to light the way to the future and to inspire people to achieve excellence**. Managers are essential to ensure that day-to-day operations run smoothly and that the assets of the corporation, both human and physical, are cared for and protected.

Obviously, it is possible for a person to have both leadership and managerial skills, and various combinations are possible. My observation, however, has been that every executive tends to favor one or the other, not both.

The role of the leader is to shepherd the operation so that everyone supports each other to achieve common objectives.

According to Harold Geneen, who led the International Telephone and Telegraph Company for seventeen years, "Leadership is the single most important ingredient in business management. Eighty to ninety percent of an organization's success is dependent on the leadership attributes of the manager to inspire his or her people to excel."[5]

The primary motivation to become a leader should be the inner satisfaction that comes from giving of yourself to create, mold, and nurture competence in a work group or organization. The size of the accomplishment is not what is important. Rather it is the creation of something of worth or value in this world. It could be as small as being a mentor for a promising young manager or as large as turning around an unprofitable company. On the other hand, when the quest for wealth, status, or the acclaim of others supersedes the inner satisfaction motive, a failure of leadership inevitably follows.

As a leader you are invested with special trust and competence to produce excellence in your organization and to ensure equity and fair treatment for all personnel. Success in this dual role does not come easily but requires considerable investment in time and energy.

Being a leader has its advantages in terms of recognition, prestige, and status. Other benefits such as higher pay and special perks are important too. Possibly the greatest reward is the feeling of self-worth that comes from being able to directly influence the course of events of an enterprise that adds value to the lives of others. With this power comes the responsibility for followers and the responsibility to achieve the goals of the organization.

The price of greatness is responsibility.
Winston Churchill

The responsibility for others—in terms of their welfare, morale, and development—cannot be overemphasized. Consider that most people spend more than one-half of their waking hours under the influence and direction of their leaders at work. For many people, work is their primary meaning in life. What an opportunity for leaders to have a positive influence in this world!

Leading others is not always easy. Certain hardships go with the benefits. First, there is the constant stress and tension of having to produce results and to be at your best. You cannot afford to let down and relax.

Prior to becoming a leader, when you were only a member of the group, you had more security. If the group did not perform well, it was not all your fault—you shared the blame with others. As a leader you cannot hide in the crowd. You are directly responsible and accountable for the results of your personnel.

Being a leader requires personal sacrifices.

Second, long hours are required of leaders both on and off the job. Eleven- and twelve-hour days are often the norm in addition to being constantly on-call after hours.

Leadership is a difficult journey.

Finally, being a leader means that you are no longer one of the "gang" and cannot maintain the same relationships with your former peers. When placed in charge, you are expected to be able to say, "No," administer discipline, and make decisions that may not be well received by some people. You face the risk of being rejected by your old friends, frequently second guessed, and talked about behind your back.

It is lonely at the top! If this bothers you, leading people may not be your "cup of tea."

Is it all worth it? That depends on your personality and desires in life. Each individual must make his own decision about being a leader by weighing the pros and cons. To me, it is all worth it and more!

II

The Challenge of Leadership

The typical business leader's world is unique since it is composed of a number of diverse special interest groups, each with its own sets of needs, expectations, and priorities (see illustration below). The leader is responsible for integrating and coordinating the functions and activities of the various groups as well as energizing each individual to do the best job possible. What makes this role such a challenge is that the leader has limited authority and control over the people with whom he interacts. Success in meeting the goals of the organization is dependent upon his ability to

secure the commitment and cooperation of everyone involved. The leader cannot dictate, order, or will that this be done. He or she must persuade and inspire others to **willingly** cooperate.

Leadership in this respect can be likened to the role of a catalyst, an agent that causes a chemical reaction when mixed with another compound. Nothing happens until the catalyst is introduced. Another analogy is that of an accomplished orchestra conductor who draws out the best efforts of his musicians to create a beautiful symphony. Without the conductor the musician's efforts would be flat and disjointed.

Obtaining commitment to a common mission from the groups that interact with the leader is difficult because many of them inherently want different things. For example, upper-management typically insists that the leader take strong measures to improve productivity. Team members, feeling overworked already would rather be left alone to focus on finding ways to make their jobs more varied and interesting. Improving productivity only for the benefit of the company turns them off.

Staff groups (i.e., Human Resources, Industrial Engineering, Quality Assurance, and Occupational Health and Safety) want the leader to give top priority to their projects or programs. The leader's spouse and children also have their own expectations, such as wanting more family time together. This may conflict with the leader's ambition to get ahead, which often requires long hours and frequent travel away from home. Obviously, the leader cannot give top priority to everything at the same time.

Except for direct reports, the leader has no formal authority over the groups that are instrumental in determining his success. Unable to obtain results by merely issuing directives, he must rely on the ability to influence and persuade.

The leaders challenge, therefore, is to convince various groups and individuals to buy into a set of common goals and then to inspire them to work together as a team to achieve those goals.

Today's unsettling workplace environment adds further complexity to the leader's mission of getting people to function effectively as a team. Due to continuous downsizing and increased focus on achieving "stretch" targets, many team members feel anxious, overworked, and exploited. These feelings often lead to negative attitudes. Overcoming these attitudes is an extremely difficult task, even for experienced leaders. Yet companies traditionally place relatively untrained people in first-level management jobs, the very positions where sound leadership can dramatically improve the work climate.

The problem of inadequate leadership at the lower levels of management has its roots in our educational system. High schools and universities do not emphasize leadership skills in the required curriculum. In addition, many young people today prefer to make money working after school rather than developing their leadership skills in extracurricular activities. They learn to take orders, not give them. The result is that most young people entering the workforce do not have an understanding of how to lead others.

In the workplace the situation is not much better since most companies do not offer pre-management training programs to prepare candidates for advancement. When promoted, the untrained individual is suddenly expected to effectively lead fifteen to twenty people in the complex social environment previously described. No wonder the leadership failure rate is so high at the first and second level of management.

Typically, first-level managers are selected for their traits of being hard-working, conscientious, and assertive. Once promoted, they usually set out to make their mark by quickly improving performance deficiencies. They often forget about the vital necessity of **first** gaining the loyalty and support of team members before making major changes.

As with most newly appointed managers, this happened to me when I joined Sealtest Foods at age twenty-two. After a short stint selling, I was given the job of managing a trucking operation in Northern

EFFECTIVE LEADERSHIP

Virginia. This branch had the worst performance record in the Eastern Region. Overtime was excessive, productivity was low, and sales volume was behind forecast. I was determined to shape things up in a hurry. Besides trying to move too quickly, I made the mistake of not involving the truck drivers in restructuring their delivery routes. As employee resentment grew, I reacted by pressing company policies even harder.

One morning when I arrived at 6:00 a.m. to observe the sort and load operation, I found the drivers milling around and talking instead of working. They decided that they had enough of my by-the-book approach and wanted to talk to the local union president and to my boss, Bill Wade. Bill, who had been a union official himself and had a good rapport with the men, persuaded them to resume work while he became involved in the issues.

That evening and well into the night, Bill counseled me until I realized that I was applying too much pressure on the men to obtain immediate results. My reaction to this insight was to let up, to be the "good guy." This, too, led nowhere. Overtime remained high and productivity low. It was not until about the seventh month on the job that I began to slowly provide the proper mix of challenging the drivers to excel and being concerned about their welfare. After a year and a half the branch became the most profitable in the region, winning an award for excellence!

There is an important lesson to be learned from this experience: **the loyalty and support of team members must be obtained before the leader attempts to implement his or her vision of the future.** This requires that the leader be patient and successfully apply the principles of effective leadership described in the following chapters.

III

The Development of Leadership Style

Before building a profile of an effective leader, I need to emphasize one point. Leaders are **made,** not born. The "born leader" school believes that a leader's style is determined by his or her genetic inheritance. The opposing viewpoint, to which I subscribe, is that leadership style is acquired in the same manner as are sophistication and graciousness—by study, emulation, and experience.

From years of participating in the development of managers, I know it is possible for individuals to shape and change their behavior. People can learn to become successful at inspiring and energizing others. Leaders are made better by first being willing to identify and understand their limitations and second by being committed to learning how to make the necessary changes in themselves.

Dwight Eisenhower was a leader who was made, not born. During World War I, when many of Eisenhower's West Point classmates were fighting and earning medals in Europe, he was stagnating in a Pentagon desk job. Shortly after the war, Eisenhower requested a transfer to Panama to work under General Fox Conner, a senior officer whom he admired. In a highly charged situation Eisenhower was tutored by his mentor in every aspect of military leadership.[1] As Eisenhower later wrote about Conner:

> *Life with General Connor was sort of a graduate school in military affairs and the humanities, leavened by a man who was experienced in his knowledge of men and their conduct. I can never adequately express my gratitude to this one gentleman. . . . In a lifetime of association with great and good men, he is the one, more or less, invisible figure to whom I owe an incalculable debt.[2]*

EFFECTIVE LEADERSHIP

With the basic premise that leadership skills are nurtured and developed during one's lifetime, let us now turn our attention to learning what effective leaders do that is worth emulating.

IV

Profile of an Effective Leader

The Central Engine Repair Shop of a major international airline was considered a managerial graveyard. Over the years a number of managers had failed to lift the shop's low productivity. With each organizational change the mechanics continued to do what they pleased—reading newspapers and magazines at their workstations, taking thirty-minute coffee breaks, and regularly washing up one-half hour before quitting time. Efforts to eliminate such practices were met with slow-downs and sick-outs.

The vice-president of Maintenance and Engineering had almost accepted this condition as a way of life when Ed Martin, an experienced, respected manager from another department, requested to be transferred to the position. When asked why he did so, he replied, "I just have a feeling that deep down, most of the guys aren't happy about the shop's poor reputation. I think I can make them feel like winners."

The first thing Ed did was to hold a meeting with the shop stewards in his office. Instead of sitting behind his desk as was customary, Ed asked them to join him at a round conference table. For several hours they talked about the problems and opportunities in the engine shop. Nothing was decided that day, but one of the union officials was later overheard saying, "I can't believe how he treated us as equals—no big-boss attitude, that's for sure." At one of the subsequent meetings a safety problem was identified that had been allowed to continue for nearly a year. In a few days Ed had the problem corrected. By continuing the dialogue and by taking strong action to resolve a number of small but potentially explosive issues, the mechanics began to gain confidence in Ed. Everyone did not agree with what was done, but there was a growing feeling in the shop that the new boss was fair and could make things happen. Next, Ed established several committees to develop suggestions for improving quality and safety. He even got a group involved in planning a baseball tournament and family cookout.

The difficult issue of adhering to break and quitting times was handled by explaining to everyone how the low productivity made it nearly impossible to win competitive bids on outside engine contract work. Additional hours for those who wanted them would be lost by not getting the business. By the time Ed put the word out that the rules and regulations would be enforced, many of the mechanics had already changed their ways. Those that did not were firmly handled on an individual basis.

By the end of Ed's first year on the job, the Engine Shop's quality and productivity results were among the best of all the shops in the Maintenance and Engineering Division. Ed knew the battle was won when he arrived one morning to find a huge banner strung across the hanger wall. It read: "We're #1."

Ulysses S. Grant faced a similar but much broader leadership challenge when Abraham Lincoln promoted him to Lieutenant General of all Northern armies in early 1864. Except for the Battle of Gettysburg, the Union had suffered decisive defeats at the hands of Robert E. Lee at Bull Run (1861 and 1862), Fredericksburg, and Chancellorsville. Grant's army was riddled with "green" draftees. Morale was poor due to inadequate leadership. In many units proper provisions were lacking.

At first, some of the troops were uncertain if the new general's name was Ulysses or Useless.[1] Then conditions slowly began to change. Equipment formerly lacking, materialized suddenly. Infantry units that had spent the war in easy jobs defending Washington,

D.C., were reassigned to the front. The cavalry, which had previously been encumbered with endless picket details, assumed an exciting new role. Now they were deployed as compact hit-and-run strike forces. A perceptible tightening-up occurred when officers began to monitor even routine jobs.[2]

Artillery units were drilled hour after hour until they achieved perfection in their maneuvers. A New England trooper best expressed the new spirit under Grant in one of his letters to home: "We all felt at last that the **boss** had arrived."[3]

Louis Gerstner, Jr., who turned around IBM, displayed the same kind of focus, intensity, and determination that Grant was so well known for. Prior to when Gerstner took over the helm at IBM in 1993, the company was in a state of disarray. Earnings had collapsed and there was talk of selling some of the major business units. Over 100,000 employees had been let go. In fact, IBM was in such poor shape that nobody, including Gerstner, was initially attracted to the job.

Fortune magazine described what happened after Gerstner arrived at IBM: "Heedless of criticism inside and outside the company, Gerstner began to cut costs, restructure, and weed out disbelievers. He jolted the culture with shock therapy. He cheer led the overhaul and revival of the mainframe, stoked the services business, and brought IBM back to the party in PC's."[4]

The Gerstner-led turnaround was impressive. After losing over 8 billion in 1993, IBM's profits surged. And the company regained the good graces of most of the customers that had previously been lost.

Successful leaders such as Ed Martin, Ulysses Grant, and Louis Gerstner act in a way that elicits the support and following of others. Their leadership qualities of focus, intensity, and determination will be as important in the future as they were in the past.

At one point in my career I thought that charisma was necessary to lead others successfully. I have since learned that charisma is helpful, but not necessary to achieve excellent results through others. Many effective leaders that I have observed seem to have little popular appeal. Their lack of charisma is usually offset by other leadership qualities, such as those presented in this book.

It should be emphasized that **real skill in leading others has to be natural and sincere.** "Techniques" contrived to manipulate people will not work. Your employees have the uncanny ability to judge the true you by your actions and deeds.

There are seventeen basic leadership attributes or qualities that are important in leading others. Together they present a profile of a leader who has compassion and consideration for his or her personnel while at the same time holding them accountable for results. Some industrial psychologists call this "tough love." The profile also includes desired personal traits of the leader, such as integrity, honesty, and morality in addition to the intangible factors of determination and courage.

There is no simple formula for leadership success. Nor is it possible to reach perfection in each leadership skill. The capacity to lead gradually builds over time. However, **one's leadership development can be accelerated by constantly visualizing the ideal leadership attributes and modeling one's own behavior after them.** These leadership attributes or qualities are presented in the next seventeen chapters. From this material you will be exposed to numerous ideas and models that will help you improve your leadership performance.

1

The Effective Leader Builds Group Cohesiveness and Pride

Deep within all of us is the desire to be a winner—to be somebody.

The fuel that runs all successful organizations is the pride and sense of accomplishment that comes from striving for and achieving high levels of performance. Employees want to be a part of a winning team. Successful teamwork is exciting, upbeat, and offers personal rewards such as status, recognition, and, in many cases, additional remuneration.

At the close of the 1984 football season Raymond Berry was hired to be interim coach of the New England Patriots, a team that had never played in a title game. In just one season the Patriots were transformed into the champions of the American Football Conference. Tackle Bryan Holloway was asked how Berry did it. His response: "Berry showed us how to win. It's like the old saying, 'If you give a man a fish, you feed him for a day. But if you show him how to catch fish, you feed him for life.' He made us believe we were the better team, and that belief can unleash awesome power when you take it out on the field with you." [1]

Early in my career at Federal Express, our president, Pete Willmott, made a visit to the truck station at Philadelphia. He was appalled by the trash and dirt on the warehouse floor, noticed a stack of brooms, picked up one, and began sweeping. The employees were so shocked that soon they were doing the same thing. Pete had made the employees aware of their lack of **pride** and attention to detail. The sloppy warehouse was indicative of the station's performance in other areas. Overtime was excessive, and the aircraft were seldom loaded on time.

Shortly after Mr. Willmott's visit, Tennyson Lewis was transferred to the Philadelphia position. It didn't take long for Tennyson to realize that the cargo handlers were dissatisfied with present conditions. Most of them felt that there was little direction and organization.

Tennyson spent the first few months getting to know the employees and learning the operation. Slowly, he began to plant the seed that the Philadelphia station could become the best in the system. This vision was a long way from the prevailing viewpoint in the company—that Philadelphia was almost a lost cause.

It was not long until the station supervisors and several respected handlers began supporting the idea of going for it—making a major performance turnaround. The thought of redeeming themselves for the sweeping incident became appealing. Pride in performance was now a part of the group's goals.

With hope for an improved future, the Philadelphia management team began making improvements everywhere. Briefings were initiated prior to each shift to review work assignments and to provide updates on what was happening in other parts of the company. New training programs began. Badly needed equipment was secured, and the office and warehouse were painted. Most importantly, management encouraged everyone to give his best and recognized each person when good work was performed.

When I visited the station a year later, the change was remarkable. The ramp crew had loaded and fueled 250 consecutive flights without delay. Not only did the Philadelphia crew take great pride in this un-

Half the battle in turning an organization around is to get people to believe that things will get better.

Compare yourself to the world's best performers in your industry, then set goals that exceed the best.
Tom Peters

usual accomplishment, but they also made sure I got a tour of their "new" facility: the same building, but with a fresh, clean look everywhere. You could have eaten off the floor!

Like Raymond Berry and Tennyson Lewis, high performing leaders do two key things to build group cohesiveness and pride. First and foremost, they establish and articulate visions of what could be for their organizations. Often these visions take the shape of "heroic goals"—possible levels of performance of such scope or magnitude that, if achieved, substantially enhance the status and prestige of the organizations. A "heroic goal" is typically one that is so remote and difficult that the leader has little or no idea how it can be achieved. All the leader has is faith and confidence that it somehow **can** be done.

Everyone likes to be a part of a winning team, especially if the team is a big winner. Going after the "heroic goal" or the ultimate level of performance creates a common mission with which everyone can identify. In baseball the ultimate achievement is winning the World Series. In horse racing it is winning the Triple Crown. Examples of "heroic goals" in the business world are obtaining the highest level of profitability in the *Fortune* 500, operating with the best level of quality in the plant, or having the lowest accident rate in the company.

The greater the obstacle, the more glory in overcoming it.

Molière

The role of the leader is to identify challenging overall objectives and to interest the organization in going after them. Edwin H. Land, founder of the Polaroid Corporation, had the right idea when he said, "The first thing you naturally do is teach the person to feel that the undertaking is manifestly important and nearly impossible."[2]

The importance of creating a feeling of ownership of the "heroic goal" cannot be overstated. It is one thing to identify a challenging goal and quite another to get people excited about going after it. If the leader tries to force the goal on his people, they will resist. Forcing change of any type makes employees feel like serfs in a feudal management kingdom—victims of management's whims. This natural feeling of resentment may not be visually apparent, but it simmers beneath the surface. Under such conditions employees go through the motions of doing the new job or task, but their hearts and souls are not in it.

How different it is when employees are **involved** in the planning stages of change and can create their own strategies for reaching the "heroic goals." When someone owns something, he or she takes better care of it. Just ask yourself: When was the last time you heard of someone waxing a rental car?

Once the "heroic goal" is identified, a good leader promotes it extensively. This important step is often neglected. **One of the secrets of effective leadership is to promote employee communications and motivational programs with the same intensity as marketing to customers.**

The best way to create employee awareness of a "heroic goal" is through symbols and slogans. To be effective they must be unusual and catchy. Two of the most successful internal advertising campaigns that I have used to promote "heroic goals" utilized such images.

The $40M Challenge. Federal Express field operating personnel were asked to be "bulldog tough" in reducing costs by $40 million during a six-month period. Posters and banners featuring a bulldog chewing on a dollar sign were used to introduce the campaign. To consistently stress the theme, weekly newsletters were published detailing individual and group cost-saving successes. Routine correspond-

All of us like to work in an environment where we can make a difference.

ence was stamped with impressions of the "dollar chewing bulldog."

A two-phase program to substantially improve service levels. First, pictures of "Mr. Good Enough," a sloppily dressed businessman, were distributed to field managers with a memo describing the philosophy that being good enough to have the best on-time delivery service in the industry was no longer acceptable. Only 100 percent achievement would be satisfactory from then on. Next, a Circle of Excellence Award Program was announced. Operating stations that achieved exceptional service levels were featured in the company newspaper and group pictures of their personnel were displayed in a glass-enclosed frame located at the corporate headquarters.

Even the best promotional efforts are of no avail unless you, the leader, continually stress goal achievement in day-to-day activities. Be enthusiastic about possibilities for improvement. Encourage creative thinking. Look for signs of progress, no matter how small. Celebrate successes. Thank those who make an extra effort. Place a premium on teamwork. You need to do all these things and much more.

In time, people will respond to your constant encouragement and enthusiasm. Before long you will be looking for another "heroic goal" that is more challenging than the first.

Tennyson Lewis, the Philadelphia station manager, did not stop when his crew achieved 250 days without an aircraft delay. When it appeared that they would go a full year without a delay, he convinced everyone that two years would be a target worthy of even more distinction. The idea is to **never be satisfied. Keep raising the sights of the organization.**

Many people working in cooperative ventures like to be energized by undertaking new challenges; they

Progress results from not being satisfied.
Frank Tyger

31

need to climb new mountains. You want your personnel to be stimulated so as to release their energy and creativity—or, in other words, to contribute at their capacity.

A word of caution about establishing "heroic goals." Be careful not to overwhelm employees by expecting too much too quickly. No one can work continuously at something without achieving some success. Good leaders break down the goal into small, obtainable pieces. The idea is to slowly build everyone's confidence—to develop the attitude of being a winner. After a few successes the group will be ready to take on the big challenge.

The second step effective leaders take to build group cohesiveness and pride is to **provide abundant feedback and recognition.** The need for frequent feedback is best illustrated by asking: How long would you continue playing tennis or golf if you couldn't keep score? Not very long. In the game of business, people need the same constant stream of information on how they are doing.

Outstanding leaders go out of their way to boost the self-esteem of their personnel. It is the key to performance improvement.

As soon as group or team performance data is available, put it on charts and graphs for everyone to see. Small improvements should be noted and encouragement offered. When good work is turned in or an extra effort made, give compliments. People thrive on praise, and the natural reaction to receiving it is to try even harder. The leader's enthusiasm for what has been accomplished is infectious. There will be a feeling of pride in meeting tough standards or goals.

David W. Johnson, who led the turnaround at the Campbell Soup Company in the 1990's, was known for the enthusiastic way that he encouraged outstanding performance from employees. When interviewed by *Investor's Business Daily,* he said: "I keep telling them (employees) we can do more. . . . I cheer them on, tell them how wonderful they are and how incredible their accomplishments are."[3]

Whenever possible, recognize outstanding performance of an individual or team in front of others. This is best done at staff meetings or at special recognition sessions. Lavish praise on those who have achieved excellence and, when appropriate, present them with a **tangible** award such as a gift certificate or a few extra days of vacation.

Purolator Courier utilizes this approach with their President's Club recognition program. Each year the top sales producers (those sales representatives who exceed quota and rank in the top 20 percent of the national sales force) are awarded an all-expense paid vacation at an exotic resort. These awards are announced with great fanfare at the national sales rally. The winners receive recognition in front of their peers plus a very attractive tangible award. This exciting program has helped Purolator create an exceptional sales force.

Intangible awards can also be highly effective in recognizing employee excellence. Years ago, I was involved in an incident that dramatically illustrates the power of simple recognition as a motivator. While serving as station manager at Newark Airport for Eastern Airlines, I sent a letter of commendation to a burly ramp serviceman named Joe to recognize his outstanding leadership in directing the unloading of a leaking package of dangerous chemicals. Had he not acted quickly and decisively, there could have been a serious aircraft fire. About two weeks after Joe received the letter, he approached me and said in his usually gruff manner, "Mr. Manske, do you know what I did with your letter?" I expected the worst, but he said, "I put it on the door of my refrigerator at home." Joe was so proud of being recognized that he posted the letter in **the** place in homes reserved for truly

What gets rewarded gets done.

important items. I had no idea that a simple letter of recognition could mean so much.

At Purolator Courier, we found a unique way of expressing appreciation for the outstanding performance of employees at the operating locations. It involves having headquarters executives and staff personnel assist the couriers on their routes on the heaviest volume day of the year (usually two days before Christmas). The objectives of the rides are to: (1) demonstrate appreciation for the excellent work done by the couriers and (2) to keep in touch with the business at the "grass roots" level. When we first started the program, some couriers were skeptical. Some thought the executives were coming out to check on them. Others thought it was a plan to introduce a new productivity program. At the end of the day, however, the couriers reported that they appreciated the recognition, but not in the way we expected. What happened was that when the customers learned who the "helpers" were, they lavished praise on the couriers. It was their way of providing a special thank you for the excellent service that the couriers provided day-in-day-out. The executive "helpers" not only learned a great deal about what happens "on the street" but also about a unique way to provide meaningful recognition.

A word of praise is far more meaningful to a person if it is related to one of his or her **qualities** (such as leadership ability, positive attitude, or honesty) than if it is tied to performance results. People like to be appreciated for their inner qualities first and then for what they produce. For example, instead of saying, "Good job on getting the XYZ account," try something more personal, such as, "I admired your determination to keep working on the XYZ account until you got the business." This approach means that you have to become familiar with the abilities and performance of

People are not motivated by failure; they are motivated by achievement and recognition.
F. F. Fournies,
Coaching for Improved Work Performance

Wherever possible, build customers into employee recognition programs.

each of your employees. It is well worth the extra effort.

Praise can be a powerful motivator if it is a sincere expression on the part of the boss and if it is related to specific, well-deserved performance accomplishments. Have you ever had a boss lavish praise on you when it was not deserved? Or, have you ever been complimented on a job when you have not even finished it? How did you feel? Not very good, I suspect. People resent receiving a pat on the back or a note saying, "Good job, keep it up," from a manager who has only a vague idea of what they do. The lesson here is obvious. Limit your praise to situations where it is deserved and where you know precisely what improvement was made.

The leader must also be careful to give credit and recognition unselfishly to those who deserve it. Don Shula, former head coach of the Miami Dolphins (two-time Super Bowl champions) did this whenever he appeared on television or at a community fund-raising dinner. He always gave his team credit for his success. Rather than "I did it," Shula said, "They did it," or, "We did it."

There is no limit to what a man can do or where he can go if he doesn't mind who gets the credit.
Author Unknown

Have you ever wondered why so many leaders obtain only marginal results in developing high levels of group cohesiveness and pride in their organizations? I believe that the lack of success has a lot to do with the size of the leader's ego. People will not respond to the vision and direction of a leader whose actions are motivated by his or her ego. Such leaders always want to be in the spotlight and take the credit for the results.

Bill Walsh, former head coach of the San Francisco 49'ers, says, *A large ego is what destroys the effectiveness of coaches. . . .The exceptional leader in any field keeps his ego in check so as not to create barriers of fear in an organization. Employees will not communicate openly and honestly if they are ridiculed when they turn out to be mistaken or if their ideas are not in line with those of the boss.* [4]

Over the years, Coach Walsh tried to remove the fear from players and assistant coaches' minds so they felt comfortable saying what they believed.[5]

In summary, to build the group cohesiveness and pride that is necessary for outstanding performance, the leader must do three essential things:

1. Establish and articulate a vision of what **could be** for the organization (i.e., establish a "heroic goal").
2. Create excitement about achieving the "heroic goal."
3. Provide abundant feedback and recognition for outstanding individual and group performance.

When the leader is able to do these three things, great accomplishments are possible because everyone becomes focused and emotionally involved.

2

The Effective Leader Lives by the Highest Standards of Honesty and Integrity

An honest man is the noblest work of God.
Alexander Pope

In the book *Profiles of Leadership,* America's top business and government leaders were asked what quality they thought was most important to their success as a leader. Their unanimous answer: **integrity.** A similar result was obtained in an American Management Association sponsored survey of 1,500 managers.[1]

Dwight D. Eisenhower had these words to say about the importance of integrity:

Honesty and integrity are best taught by example.

> *In order to be a leader a man must have followers. And to have followers, a man must have their confidence. Hence the supreme quality for a leader is unquestionably integrity. Without it, no real success is possible, no matter whether it is on a section gang, a football field, in an army, or in an office. If a man's associates find him guilty of phoniness, if they find that he lacks forthright integrity, he will fail. His teachings and action must square with each other. The first great need, therefore, is integrity and high purpose.[2]*

It is one thing to **talk** about integrity and honesty, and it is quite another to **live** your life that way. The true test of honesty is a truthful answer to this question: *Would you return money that was given to you in error (say, by a bank teller or store cashier) when you knew you had the opportunity to keep it without being caught?*

At a large retailing company, thirty-five senior executives were given a paper and pencil honesty test. Prior to the test, they were guaranteed absolute anonymity. The results: two-thirds of the executives admitted that they occasionally falsified their expense accounts.[3]

In just one recent year three *Fortune* 500 companies pleaded guilty to crimes ranging from fraud to issue of false claims for government contract expenses. In addition, the chairmen of the board of two large industrial firms, a bank president, and a defense contractor were sentenced to jail terms for misuse of company funds and obstruction of justice. Only a few months after these scandals, Wall Street was rocked with the arrest of several high-level officials from the leading stock brokerage firms for alleged insider trading abuses.

These and other disturbing incidences of high-level leaders acting as if they were above the law present poor examples for those aspiring to reach the top.

Corruption and dishonesty seem to occur when the leader loses sight of the fact that he or she is given power for one purpose—to serve others. Harry Truman put it another way: "If a man can accept a situation in a place of power with the thought that it's only temporary, he comes out all right. But when he thinks he is the cause of the power, that can be his ruination."

W. F. Smith, a noted Dallas businessman, goes a step further with his concept of power. He says that **"Power for good flows through you from God. It does not originate with you."** In other words, you are not the source of power, but a conduit through

> *The greatest contribution leaders can make to mankind is to use their power in a positive way—to help and inspire others.*

> *Aggrogance, brought about by a feeling of superiority over others, is one of the worst traits a leader can have.*

which it flows. Maintaining one's humility should never be a problem for a leader if he or she keeps Mr. Smith's viewpoint in mind.

Besides maintaining a proper perspective about their power, leaders must be careful not to place too much pressure on their personnel to achieve unrealistic "stretch" targets. When subordinates realize that the only way to make targets is to cut corners, the seeds for unethical behavior are sown. Some employees who are unable to cope with the consequences of failure will grasp at anything to retain their good standing in the organization—such as falsifying reports or purposely violating corporate policies.

More than anything else, followers want to believe that their leaders are ethical and honest. They want to say, "Someday I want to be like him or her."

The development of highly principled leaders is vitally important to the future of any organization. In a broader sense it is imperative for the future of our country. This is why I always close my leadership seminars or speeches with the following exhortation:

If you would remember only one thing from this presentation let it be: Live your life by the highest standards of honesty and integrity. Throughout your career you will be tempted to do the expedient, to shade the truth, or violate ethical principles. Stand firm, don't waiver, and someday you can look back at your accomplishments with pride and satisfaction, for you will have succeeded by doing things the right way without violating the trust given to you by your associates. More than anything else, your legacy will be that you inspired others to live their lives in a similar fashion.

Integrity is not a given in everyone's life. It is the result of self-discipline, inner trust, and a decision to be relentlessly honest in all situations in our lives.
1987 Workman Page-A-Day Calendar

*A good name is seldom regained. When **character** is gone, one of the richest jewels of life is lost forever.*
J. Hanes

Integrity in a leader must be **demonstrated** daily and in a number of tangible ways:

1. **Do what you say you will do.** If you promise something to an employee or colleague, keep your word. Never hint at a possible future award to sugarcoat an unpleasant decision.

   The Center for Creative Leadership in Greensboro, North Carolina, conducted a study of twenty-one high-potential executives who were terminated or forced to retire early from their companies. The one universal character flaw or unforgivable sin that always led to downfall was betraying a trust—not doing something that was promised.[4]

2. **Never divulge information given in confidence to you** unless required by law to do so.

3. **Accept responsibility for your mistakes.** Every successful executive has made his or her share of mistakes. The trouble is that many people will not own up to them. Do not be afraid to say, "I made a mistake."

   The other day one of my associates missed an important meeting. When I asked him about it, he surprised me by saying, "I just forgot. I won't make that mistake again." No other excuses were offered. My first thought was, "How refreshing."

   Jack Welch, the exceptional CEO of General Electric for over a decade, admitted in his book *Control Your Destiny or Someone Else Will* that he made plenty of mistakes over the years. They did not ruin him because he was not averse to accepting blame for poor decisions.

   If you do make a major mistake, confront it head-on. Don't try to cover it up or minimize it. Instead, immediately own up to it with your boss.

The problem is that most leaders today don't stand for anything. If you don't stand for something, you'll fall for anything.
Don Shula
Everyone's a Coach

Indicate that you accept full responsibility for the blunder and that you will develop a plan for ensuring that it never happens again. Then take decisive corrective action, keeping everyone informed of your progress. Leaders that utilize this approach when they make a major mistake will normally minimize or avoid damage to their careers. In some cases one's career could actually be enhanced as the mistake provides an opportunity to demonstrate several valued leadership attributes: 1) courage, 2) willingness to accept responsibility, and 3) decisiveness.

Every time people engage in dishonest or immoral acts, the results come back to haunt them.

4. **Never become involved in a falsehood or a lie.** If your employees ever catch you misrepresenting the facts, lying to them, or covering up a problem, you will lose credibility instantly. And it will not be easy to regain.

    Dr. William Schultz, a noted psychologist who developed truth-in-management strategies at Proctor and Gamble and NASA, believes the key to productivity is "how well people work together and that nothing increases compatibility like mutual trust and honesty."[5] He continues by saying, "If people in business just told the truth, 80 to 90% of their problems would disappear."[6] Trust and honesty then become the means that allow individuals to cooperate so that they can all prosper.

There is no pillow as soft as a clear conscience.
John Wooden

5. **Avoid accepting gifts from suppliers.** This is an area where I have seen a number of capable young managers go astray. Problems usually begin when they accept gifts from a supplier at Christmas. Soon they are being entertained at a lavish resort for a weekend. It is not hard to imagine what happens after that.

The key question you must always ask yourself: "What is the right thing to do?"

Maintaining high standards of honesty and integrity in today's business world takes an inner toughness and resolve to persevere, often under extreme pressure or even under the threat of losing your job. Situations may arise when superiors expect you to do something unethical, dishonest, or even illegal. It may be an order to keep quiet about a safety flaw in a product, a demand to alter financial statements, or a request not to report an accident. Torn between upholding your values and loyalty to superiors, you must make a choice. You can compromise yourself by doing the expedient, or you can stand up for what you believe and take the consequences. In the long run you are always better off to **do what is right.**

Having a free conscience is important to being able to live with yourself. One can take great pride in saying, "I made it without cheating or undermining others." Ethical business leaders are in demand in the marketplace. Therefore, do not waste valuable career time in organizations that do not revere high values.

Trust is the ultimate meaning of success.
Dean Witter
Advertisement

The true measure of living your life by the highest standards of honesty and integrity comes if you can go any place in the world and never encounter someone who can point a finger at you and say, "That man is a liar and a cheat!"

Remember, **without integrity you do not have trust, and without trust you have nothing!**

The Three-Way Test to Determine If a Decision or Action Is Ethical

I. **DOES IT VIOLATE ANY LAWS OR COMPANY POLICIES?**[7]

II. **IS IT FAIR TO ALL CONCERNED?**[8]

III. **AM I PROUD OF IT — PROUD ENOUGH TO TELL MY FAMILY AND FRIENDS ABOUT IT?**[9]

For a decision or action to be considered ethical, the answer to question number one should be "no" and the answers to questions two and three should be "yes." A different answer to any of the questions should serve as a red light; stop and reconsider your decision or plan.

3

The Effective Leader Shares Information Openly and Willingly

From years of talking to employees throughout the world I find they all share the common desire to be "in the know." They want to be taken into confidence about where their company is headed and how future plans might affect them. Clear answers must be provided to "what's in it for me" questions, such as what will be gained in terms of status, pay, learning opportunities and job satisfaction.

It is not important that everyone understands all the details of the company's strategies. A general understanding will do. The point is that by taking the time to share information, the leader demonstrates that he or she values the individual as an important member of the organization.

Sharing information about goals and strategies is very important to the success of an organization. People need to know where they are headed before they can make commitments to place group needs above their own.

It has been my experience in dealing with both nonunion and union groups that it is advantageous to share financial information, both good and bad, with employees. The worst thing you can do to people is to keep them in the dark. If your company is doing well, employees at all levels need to know that they have been successful. This is necessary to build their company pride. If the company is experiencing financial difficulties, employees also need to know the facts so they can effectively participate in solving the problems. In his book *Made In America,* Sam Walton adds: "The gain you receive from communicating everything you possibly can to associates more than offsets the risk of informing your competitors."

What employees **do not** want is a lot of formal corporate communication, such as newspapers or letters from top management. These forms of communications tend to be impersonal and rarely address the real issues on the front line. Everyone wants the straight scoop without all of the embellishments and carefully chosen words that typify most communications from headquarters. **What is most desired is frequent, candid information from the immediate manager.**

When I was the Newark Airport station manager for Eastern Airlines, I had a very capable ramp manager named Tom Chuchran. Tom had a difficult job in that he was responsible for motivating several hundred ramp servicemen who loaded and unloaded passenger luggage all day. Because of the repetitious nature of the work, there was a tendency to be lackadaisical in sorting bags to the proper connecting flights. To complicate matters, Tom's personnel were represented by a strong union.

The finest expression of respect is not praise or status, but a willingness to talk openly to a person.
Less Bittle, Author & Editor, McGraw Hill Publishing Co.

For several years I had the opportunity to observe, first-hand, Tom's exceptional style of personal communications. Tom spent most of the day talking to his men one-on-one or in small groups. He once told me that he made it a point to see all of his team at least once a day. This was not an easy task since the operation ran from 6:00 a.m. until midnight.

More than anything else, Tom was sincerely interested in the welfare of each person. He made it a point to keep track of employee illnesses and serious personal problems. If an individual was sick in the hospital, Tom went out of his way to visit him. On more than one occasion he loaned money to a person with a serious financial problem.

Tom always seemed to be available to answer questions about the operation or to lend a hand when needed. When each shift punched in, he was present in the ready room. At break time he often could be seen drinking coffee with his men. Even at the end of the day Tom was available to anyone who wanted to talk. Often he accompanied one or two employees to their cars after work.

The Newark employees viewed Tom as a trusted source of information about the company. If a question was raised that he could not answer, he would admit that he did not know, but would find out. I do not recall Tom ever failing to keep such a promise. Around the airport it was said that if you wanted to get the straight scoop, just ask Tom.

Let us examine Tom's communication style to see why it was so effective. Foremost, he was in constant touch with his personnel, sharing and disseminating information. Tom instinctively knew that the major reason for poor communications is the assumption that everyone understands what to do and why. He therefore went out of his way to carefully explain new directives—especially the reasons and rationale for them. Information about future plans was readily given. For example, if discussions were being held at headquarters concerning possible flight increases or cutbacks at Newark, employees were kept appraised. No one therefore felt a need to develop a rumor mill.

The basic building block of good communications is the feeling that every human being is unique and of value.

Disruptive rumors never had a chance to get off the ground.

Tom's ramp servicemen responded to the concern and attention shown them by being open and candid in return. They had ample opportunities to get things off their chests without resorting to more drastic measures. Such freedom of expression enabled Tom to clear up misunderstandings and minor irritations before they developed into formal grievances.

More than once, Tom Chuchran's intimate style of communication saved the day for Eastern at Newark Airport. On one cold winter night the termination of an employee led to a slowdown in baggage handling. Passengers were waiting two hours for their luggage. Only because of their respect and trust for Tom was everyone persuaded to resume their normal pace of work.

4

The Effective Leader Coaches to Improve Performance

It is only as we develop others that we succeed.
H. S. Firestone

The most important responsibility of a leader is to develop people. Your success as a leader is dependent upon how well your personnel perform. One of the reasons managers are not promoted is that they do not have someone ready to replace them. It is therefore in your best interest to **make employee development your number one priority.**

The ultimate leader is one who is willing to develop individuals to the point that they eventually surpass him or her in knowledge and ability. This generative process is necessary for the long-term prosperity of the company.

There are two prerequisites for personal development to occur. First, there must be a supportive environment for learning. Second, the individual must want to learn.

Create the kind of climate in your organization where personal growth is expected and rewarded.

In a supportive learning environment the leader-coach encourages employees to try new things and take calculated risks to improve performance. Personal growth will not occur unless experimentation is fostered. Under such conditions employees will make mistakes. The important element is how the leader reacts to them. If he or she accepts honest mistakes as the price for innovation, employees will not be afraid to keep seeking better ways of doing things. In such an environment the focus is always on what can be learned from the failure. In effect, mistakes become "stepping stones" to success.

One of the first jobs I had after graduating from college was purchasing trucks for Sealtest Foods. One day after spending considerable time reviewing bids for a sizable order of tractor-trailers, I made a recommendation to the director of purchasing that we award the contract to Ford. After a verbal order was placed with Ford I discovered a mistake in my computations; another company offered more value for the same price. I will never forget the day I made my way to the director's office to inform him of my mistake. I can even recall the overcast sky that day and the dark gray color of the rug in the elevator. After I nervously confessed my error, the director sat back in his chair and reflected for what seemed like an eternity. Finally, he said, "I'm disappointed in the quality of your work on this project, but all is not lost if you learned something." Rather than make me feel foolish and incompetent, he expressed confidence that I would be more thorough with the next bid.

This incident had a lasting impression on my life. I decided at that time that I would always make **quality,** not speed, the most important consideration in my work.

One evening I visited the Long Beach station of Federal Express just as the couriers were returning from their routes. I watched with interest as the managers helped the couriers unload their trucks. While sharing the work tasks of the evening, the managers encouraged the couriers to talk about the good and the bad events of the day. What a creative way to demonstrate empathy and concern and to learn about the problems they encountered.

The second prerequisite for building personal development is the readiness of the individual. The individual must want to improve his knowledge and

If your personnel aren't making an occasional mistake or two, it's a sure sign they're playing it too safe.

Those who believe in our ability do more than stimulate us; they create for us an atmosphere in which it becomes easier to succeed.
John H. Spalding

49

skills. The drive to learn and improve can only come from within the person. No one can force an individual to pay attention and absorb new material.

The leader-coach can influence this drive by the example he sets in his own developmental practices and by his belief in the trainee's capacity for growth. If someone believes in you, it is a powerful incentive for you to live up to that belief. A story from my youth illustrates this important point. After my junior high school graduation my homeroom teacher came up to me to offer her congratulations. Her parting words went something like this: "Fred, you've had a great year, and all the teachers, including myself, are proud of your accomplishments. We know you'll do well in senior high." With such an expression of confidence in me, how could I do anything but try my best in the future?

Confidence building is what coaching is all about.

With a supportive environment for learning firmly established in the organization and a willingness to learn on the individual's part, it is now up to the leader-coach to guide and facilitate employee performance improvement by (1) asking the proper questions, (2) encouraging and reinforcing behavioral change, and (3) providing an example of excellence for others to follow.

Encourage your personnel to explore new options instead of settling for the obvious.

Good coaches know that real learning does not occur unless people are challenged to do their own thinking—to come up with their own ideas and solutions to problems without being given the answers.

The best way to stimulate such growth in your subordinates is to ask them open-ended questions that require thoughtful responses. Here are a few samples. I am sure you can think of many more.

- What are your recommendations?
- What do you think?
- Could the job be done a better way?
- What's not quite right in your operation?

- What are you planning to do?
- What do you want to accomplish during the next six months?

Notice that none of these questions elicits a defensive reaction. Neither do they make the person feel dependent on the coach for his knowledge and expertise. Rather, they focus the discussion on the employee's thoughts and ideas, thereby developing his ability to think and make decisions. Contrast this developmental approach with one that is authoritative, as illustrated by the boss saying, "Your overtime is out of control; start cutting hours immediately!" or "The solution to your absenteeism problem is to give warning letters to the worst offenders."

How different it is when the employees come up with their own solutions. Their commitment and the intensity of their action will be far stronger when such employee ownership exists than if they merely carry out the manager's precise directives. This does not mean that the manager should not coax or lead the employee in a certain direction. This is often necessary to avoid costly mistakes.

The use of the question, "What do you want to accomplish during the next six months?" is an excellent way for the manager to start an employee appraisal. It immediately focuses attention on the employee's plans for improving performance rather than dwelling on past failures and mistakes. Tension and defensiveness are minimized, thereby opening minds for consideration of **what could be.** As the discussion of future possibilities continues, the employee will invariably identify his own deficiencies. It is at this point that the appraiser can add his own perspective by pointing out other areas that require improvement.

According to F. F. Fournies, writing in *Coaching for Improved Work Performance,* there are four common

The role of the coach is to teach his players to stand on their own feet.

Good leadership consists in showing average people how to do the work of superior people.
John D. Rockefeller

reasons why people do not perform the way they should:

1. They do not know **what** they are supposed to do.
2. They do not know **how** to do it.
3. They do not know **why** they should.
4. There are obstacles beyond their control.

Occasionally, there is a fifth reason for unsatisfactory performance: the person does not care enough to do the job properly. In other words, he has an attitude problem.

Fortunately, most people want to do a good job. When the leader asks the proper questions, he or she can quickly ascertain which areas of performance are deficient. Corrective action can then be taken by providing counseling or, if necessary, retraining.

The second way the leader-coach influences employee performance is by encouraging and reinforcing behavioral change. An individual's behavior on the job is often directly related to his or her attitude. I have found that few performance problems occur when the person has a strong work ethic and cares about doing a good job. On the other hand, if the individual has an attitude problem, you are faced with the difficult challenge of trying to change what the person cares about or what he believes. At this point the stakes are high, for if you cannot stimulate change for the better, you may have to discharge the individual.

People can adapt or change their attitudes if the inner motivation to do so is there. Acting as the catalyst for such change is one of the most difficult aspects of leadership. How does a leader facilitate positive changes in an individual's behavior that comes from a poor attitude?

Start by being frank and honest with the individual about what he or she is doing. Make sure your feedback is based on what you observed rather than secondhand information. Honesty does not mean being brutal. It means indicating your displeasure about the deficiency in a firm, nonthreatening manner. For example, a cavalier attitude about attending meetings on time could be handled like this: "Joan, you have arrived late to our last two meetings. This is causing everyone to lose valuable time waiting for you. This behavior is unacceptable."

Unacceptable performance must not go unchallenged.

Never criticize the personal qualities of the individual, such as his integrity, character or intelligence; criticize only the unsatisfactory quality of the work or the inappropriate action taken.

Good coaches do not dwell long on the statement of the performance deficiency. After firmly expressing their concern they immediately begin to ask probing questions to ascertain what is causing the adverse behavior. The objective here is to reach agreement with the employee on the root causes. Now the coach can involve the individual in problem solving. The ideal situation is to get him to reach his own conclusions on how to improve in the future. Always conclude such coaching with a strong effort to keep the relationship with the employee intact. One of the approaches I use is to let the person know that I am offering the feedback so he can do a better job in the future. You want the individual to leave the coaching session with the feeling that you care enough about him to have risked confrontation and rejection for the purpose of helping him develop. It was T. S. Eliot who said: "The mark of a great critic is one who brings to a situation, not one who takes something away."[1]

Caring is at the heart of good coaching.

The hardest part of leadership is being candid with people about performance deficiencies. Many managers fail miserably in this area because they wish to avoid conflict. Instead of dealing directly with the performance problems, they pass over them or treat them lightly in performance reviews. The result: no

People prefer a leader who gives them the straight facts—good and bad.

one wins. The employee does not receive the feedback that is necessary to improve; the manager does not get the excellence that is desired; and the company continues to be stuck with a marginal performer.

Knowing where you stand with your manager is a universal need of every employee. This is best illustrated by the comments of a Southwest Airlines employee in Texas: "The boss should tell you right away when you're doing wrong. A person wants to know this so he has an opportunity to correct the problem before it's too late."

Knowing where you stand with your boss is related to the basic human need for security. Your personnel expect you to help them feel secure in their jobs; it is difficult to perform well when one expects a dismissal notice at any moment. Fearful employees are less productive in their jobs because they spend too much time and energy worrying about what their manager thinks about them. It is only when they feel secure that they can release their imaginations and creative energies.

Normally, a frank performance discussion clears the air for both the leader and the employee. The leader has gotten an important matter off his chest that may have been bothering him for some time. The employee becomes aware of his shortcomings, has an opportunity to express his viewpoints, and becomes involved in solving the problem. He realizes that his boss is displeased and expects improvement. The stage is now set for positive change.

After such performance counseling most people will make some effort, albeit small, to improve. Because even supportive feedback can make employees cautious, the initial improvement may hardly be noticeable. The employee is testing the water to see what happens. Here is a great opportunity for the leader-coach. If this initial effort to improve—as small as it may be—is noticed and recognized in a sincere way, the employee will try even harder the next time.

Giving encouragement to do even better can be a powerful stimulant for further improvement. Mary Kay Ash, the founder of Mary Kay Cosmetics, used this positive reinforcement approach with her employees. She said, "Forget their mistakes and zero in on one small thing they do right. Praise them and they'll do more things right and discover talents and abilities they never realized they had."[2]

The third way the leader-coach influences employee performance improvement is by setting an example. If the leader does not give his best, especially by demonstrating hard work and excellence, how can he expect subordinates to do more?

Example is the school of mankind and they will learn at no other.
Edmund Burke

When I was in the Coast Guard, I served on two cutters. On the first ship the officers worked a minimal number of hours. They spent most of the day in the officers' mess reading magazines and drinking coffee. The crew responded in kind. We made a game of seeing how little work we could do without getting caught. Elaborate communication systems were developed to signal the approach of an officer when it was time for inspection.

Our attitude on the second ship was entirely different. There we voluntarily worked overtime and took great pride in our work. It was the same enlisted crew on both ships. The officers, not the crew, made the difference. On the second ship they set the example by working hard, long hours. Little of their time was spent drinking coffee. Instead, the officers dedicated themselves to supporting our efforts by ensuring we had proper equipment and supplies. They went out of their way to encourage us and reward good performance. We always seemed to have the best food and latest movies of all the ships in the Atlantic fleet.

There is no more noble occupation in the world than to assist another human being—to help someone succeed.

Alan Loy McGinnis
Bringing Out the Best in People

What happens if after setting a positive example, you still are unable to inspire the poor performer to change for the better? This is when you should employ the disciplinary approach as outlined in chapter 7.

As you begin your task of improving your coaching performance by asking the proper questions, encouraging and reinforcing behavioral change, and by setting an example of excellence, keep in mind that the payoff is great. Besides contributing to the success of your organization, you will have participated in the most satisfying part of any leader's job—the growth and development of people. This is the highest calling of leadership. **In my opinion, there is no greater monument at the end of one's career than the performance of those individuals who have reached their fullest potential because of your leadership.**

5

The Effective Leader Insists on Excellence

Great leaders are never satisfied with current levels of performance. They constantly strive for higher and higher levels of achievement.

In my office I keep a sketch of a sloppily dressed businessman with a button on his jacket reading "Mr. Good Enough." The drawing is titled: "The Enemy of Excellence." Good enough is the enemy of excellence! When excellence is defined as zero defects, error-free paperwork processing, or 100% on-time servicing of customers, any other performance level is unacceptable.

For years in America the prime example of the "good enough" philosophy was the 95% quality standard. Many manufacturing companies consciously established rejection rates at 5%. Executives believed this was a tolerable level for customers and a way to avoid substantial additional costs. The problem is that the Japanese changed the rules by deciding to compete on price **and** quality. While most American firms rested on their laurels at a 95% quality rate, the Japanese were busy finding ways to improve it to 97%, 99% and ultimately to 100%.

This philosophy of excellence is described in *Toyotas Basic Management Handbook:*

Excellence is best described as doing the right things right.

> *The only acceptable quality percentage is 100%. Every car must be manufactured exactly according to specifications. No Toyota should ever leave the factory without passing quality tests perfectly.[1]*

EFFECTIVE LEADERSHIP

Breaking through the "good enough" barrier to enter the zone of excellence requires total preoccupation with quality from everyone in the organization. It starts with the leader's attitude. If he or she insists on excellence, it will more than likely be obtained. This is called a "self-fulfilling prophecy."

In a classroom experiment with grade school children, one teacher was told she had a group of "spurters"—those that had a strong potential for high academic achievement. The truth was that they were average. Another teacher was told she had a group of slow learners. Actually, they were also average. The result of the experiment: the "spurters" progressed much more rapidly than the "slow" group.[2]

The intelligence level of both groups was the same. What made the performance difference was how the teachers related to their students. Each teacher had a different expectation of how the children would perform and treated them accordingly. The "spurters" reponded to their teacher's high expectations by paying more attention in class and studying harder at home. The children in the second group became bored with the slow, repetitious nature of the instruction.[3]

The people in my life for whom I have the most gratitude (such as my parents; an Ohio Wesleyan University professor, Libby Reed; and my first boss, Bill Wade) expected a great deal from me and pushed me relentlessly toward excellence. At times I certainly did not appreciate their interest in me, but now I realize that they cared enough to challenge me.

Effective leaders bring out the best in people by stimulating them to achieve what they thought was impossible.

Expect the best and you will get it!

Often, however, merely expecting the best is insufficient to obtain desired results. People frequently need to be shown that the seemingly impossible performance level is possible.

For years no one believed it possible to run the mile race under four minutes. Until 1954, the best time ever was 4:01.4 by Gunder Haegg in 1945. Conventional wisdom held that the heart just could not stand the added stress of running any faster. Then Roger Bannister proved it could be done with a shocking time of 3:59.4. In a short time period thereafter twenty-six different men broke the four minute barrier.[4]

Similarly in 1984, the Federal Express field organization was having difficulty improving the accuracy of airbill documents. Airbill accuracy was important because the data from it was used to prepare customer invoices, but the error rate continuously hovered around 10% no matter how much pressure was exerted on the managers.

Finally, out of sheer frustration, I decided to try a new approach. I called one of our regional directors and asked him to do a favor for me. He said, "What's on your mind?" I replied, "The airbill error rate is really hurting us system wide. Would you please take the Chicago operation and ask the employees there to figure out a way to improve the accuracy to at least 98%. When you succeed, I'd like to use their approach as the model for the entire system."

In about forty-five days the director called and said, "I've got good news! We did it even better than you asked; we've increased the accuracy rate to nearly 100%."

When the other regional directors learned of the big breakthrough in Chicago, it wasn't long before the system error rate improved from 10% to .5%.

Besides showing people that major turnarounds in performance are possible, **the leader should set the example for excellence in everything that he or she does.** Employees will not respond to requests for better and better results from a leader who does not expect the same from himself or herself.

Here are a few additional tips for securing excellence in your organization:

1. **Become obsessed with high-quality achievement.** This means that you constantly make quality improvement your number one priority.

   Over the years I have seen many quality improvement programs come and go. Most of them had short lives. Those that were successful in the long run had one common denominator—leaders who day-in-day-out stressed quality above everything else.

2. **Recognize and make heroes out of employees who achieve exceptional quality results.** Soon other employees will emulate the heroes' behaviors. (Review chapter 1 for specific ways to reward high achievers.)

3. **Attack the root causes of poor quality.** Why is it so important to attack the root causes or fundamental reasons for poor quality? The answer is that it is far less costly to do the job right the first time than to fix the problem later. For example, it only takes a moment for the courier to check the accuracy of the airbill at the point of pickup. At this time the customer is usually available to straighten out any errors or misunderstandings. Attempting to do this at a later date involves expensive telephone and clerical time plus the possible loss of customer goodwill.

   In auto manufacturing the elimination of a production defect on the assembly line may cost $2- $5 a car. If the dealer has to make good on the defect, the cost could easily reach $50. The lesson here is obvious—**take whatever actions are necessary to do the job right the first time.**

Techniques for Achieving Excellence from Effective Leadership

I.   MAKE QUALITY YOUR NUMBER ONE PRIORITY.

II.   DEFINE EXCELLENCE AS ZERO DEFECTS, ZERO ERRORS, AND ZERO FAILURES.

III.   INVOLVE EVERYONE IN PLANNING AND IMPLEMENTING QUALITY IMPROVEMENTS.

IV.   SHOW TEAM MEMBERS HOW TO ACHIEVE EXCELLENCE.

V.   INSIST ON EXCELLENCE.

VI.   SET THE EXAMPLE FOR EXCELLENCE.

VII.   MAKE HEROES OUT OF EMPLOYEES WHO ACHIEVE EXCEPTIONAL RESULTS.

VIII.   ATTACK THE ROOT CAUSES OF POOR QUALITY.

IX.   ALWAYS ATTEMPT TO DO THE JOB RIGHT THE FIRST TIME.

6

The Effective Leader Sets the Example for Others to Follow

People are changed, not by coercion or intimidation, but by example.

Several days after addressing our Western Region managers on the topic of leadership, I received a note from one of the participants thanking me for inspiring him. He closed by saying, "I've always admired your style of total integrity, rigidity of purpose, and your being a good family man and a gentleman. To these qualities do I aspire as a future executive."

Prior to receiving the manager's letter, I had not fully realized the extent to which leaders influence and shape the attitudes and behavior of their followers. Most ambitious young people desire to someday reach the top of their organizations. They will model their behavior after what they observe in their leaders. If their leaders demonstrate high levels of honesty, integrity, and teamwork, subordinates will consider these traits necessary for success and will act accordingly.

Example is not the main thing in influencing others. It is the only thing.
Albert Schweitzer

My mother once told me something that I will never forget. She said, "Fred, by your deeds you will be known." What she was saying was that **what you do as a leader exerts far more influence on followers than what you say.**

Around your employees you are constantly on stage. Everything you do is interpreted as acceptable behavior for them to emulate. If you work hard and are conscientious, others will follow suit. If you follow the rules and adhere to the organization's policies, your people will be encouraged to do the same.

As the leader you should try to remain upbeat even during difficult times. But, no one expects you to **always** be stoic and never show your emotions. Leaders, like everyone else, experience negative feelings brought on by disappointment and fear of failure. It's not bad for your personnel to occasionally see you in a "down" mood. This lets them know that you're human too. Ken Blanchard, writing in *Everyone's a Coach,* says, "One of the most destructive traits that a leader can have is arrogance—acting like you've got it all together all the time." However, a leader cannot afford to be "down" for long periods of time or be considered moody. When this happens, employee morale suffers.

In short, the example you set, both positive and negative, will establish the standards for your organization. What are some of the ways you can set an example worth emulating by your people?

Commitment is the stuff character is made of—the power to change the face of things.[1]

1. **Become totally committed to doing the best job possible.** Throw yourself into your work. Perform assignments with a high degree of enthusiasm. Do more than you are asked—even if it involves some personal inconvenience, such as occasionally working at night or on a weekend.

   Lou Holtz, one of the winningest college football coaches ever, recalls that in the early part of his career he accepted the top position with the New York Jets without being totally committed to taking the Jets to the Super Bowl. The result was that the Jets failed miserably, and he was released after eight months.

   Barbara Jordan, the first black congresswoman from Texas, said, "Each day you have to look into the mirror and say to yourself, 'I'm going to be the best I can no matter what it takes.'"

Sam Walton, the founder of Wal-Mart, was noted for his strong work ethic. He once said, "Commit to your business. I think I overcame every single one of my shortcomings by the sheer passion I brought to my work."

2. **Build your team with the highest quality people** — not only in terms of their knowledge and skills, but their morals and integrity. Put them in key positions where they can be the greatest help in building an organization culture known for its professionalism and ethics. I have always felt that the true measure of a leader is the quality of people he selects as team members.

3. **Maintain a cheerful pleasant attitude.** This is one of the finest things you can do for your personnel. It sets the tone for how they should treat each other. President Eisenhower, with his boyish grin, had a knack for getting people to do what he wanted without appearing gruff or upset. I am convinced that you can be just as decisive and firm with a pleasant look on your face as you can with a scowl.

4. **Refrain from "passing the heat" up to your superiors** when you have a disagreeable job to do, such as introducing an unpopular new policy or program. A weak leader will try to avoid the criticism of his or her personnel by saying, "I had no choice in the matter," or "This came down from headquarters, and they're insisting it be done." As a member of management, it is the leader's job to fully understand the reasons for new policies and procedures and to effectively sell them in an empathic but firm manner, avoiding all reference to who requested the change.

5. **Be willing to say, "I made a mistake" or "I don't know."** If you criticize an employee and later discover that he was right, you should immediately go to that person and apologize for your error.

Thomas Watson, Jr., the former chairman of IBM, on one occasion went so far as to go from his office to a person's home to apologize for an insult.[2]

Executives who are unable to own up to mistakes place their welfare above that of the company. They have the mistaken belief that somehow they will lose their status and respect if they reveal an imperfection. They seem to be compelled to be infallible.

There are no mistakes so great as that of being always right.
Samuel Butler

There is something refreshing and appealing about an executive who occasionally makes himself vulnerable to criticism by saying, "I was wrong," or "I don't know." Besides, being defensive and always trying to prove you are right wastes valuable energy that could be more appropriately deployed in a positive manner.

One trait that made Abraham Lincoln a great leader was his open-mindedness and willingness to admit his mistakes. Unlike people who react defensively, Lincoln had a high degree of self-confidence and humility that enabled him, when necessary, to change course or reverse himself. During the Civil War he signed a directive to transfer several regiments from one battle sector to another. When Edwin M. Stanton, the Secretary Of War, heard about the order, he refused to obey it, saying, "Lincoln is a damn fool." When Stanton's remark was passed on to Lincoln, he reacted by acknowledging, "I must be wrong because Stanton is far more knowledgeable in military matters." Later Lincoln met with Stanton and reversed the order.[3]

Most young managers interested in developing themselves are thirsty to learn from the experiences of respected leaders. Of particular interest are the details of the errors that these role models made and what was learned from them. Instead of being secretive about the past, leaders should talk openly and honestly about it. Anecdotes of victories and failures can give hope and encouragement to employees faced with difficult leadership problems.

6. **Avoid indiscreet, negative criticism of colleagues.** In other words, be loyal. No matter how disloyal you feel, never express it. You can expect that even a mildly critical statement about an associate will eventually get back to him or her.

How easy it is to sit back and criticize the performance of another person or department! Yet, it is quite another thing to make positive suggestions for improvement. Will Rogers summed it all up by saying, "There is nothing as easy as denouncing. It don't take much to see that something is wrong, but it does take some eyesight to see what will put it right again." Therefore, avoid participating in conversations that focus on how bad things are in other areas of the company. Instead, put all your energy into making your department or section the best.

7. **Work hard and smart.** Most outstanding leaders not only work hard, but also have a knack of working on the right activities. They always have an agenda of important tasks they want to accomplish each day. And the important areas are related to the overall objectives of their companies and the priorities of their departments. For more information on how to work smart by focusing your attention and making every minute count, refer to chapter 12.

One universal trait that distinguishes leaders from followers is their level of energy. Leaders seem to possess enormous amounts of it. The average person works from forty to forty-five hours a week and comes home to a leisurely dinner and

Resolve that whatever you do you will bring the whole man to it; that you will fling the whole weight of your being into it.

Orison S. Marden

several hours of television. Leaders usually spend fifty-to-sixty hours at the office, frequently attend company and civic functions at night, and devote numerous leisure hours to reading journals and books that broaden their horizons.

8. **Never get involved in the dark side of office politics,** such as maligning associates, practicing deceit, manipulating others or withholding information to enhance your position. Although you may be successful in doing these things for a while, it will not take long for your colleagues to identify your true nature and turn against you. However, it is natural and normal to be an active participant in the political process that occurs in every organization, which involves trying to influence others, networking, and exercising power.

The issue, therefore, is not the degree of involvement in office politics, but how you play the game. If you strive to unselfishly assist coworkers, stay on congenial terms with them, and refrain from the dark side of politics, you **can** exert influence without compromising your ethics. Moreover, the example you set will encourage others to follow suit.

9. **Stand up for the principles you believe in.** People trust leaders who make known their convictions and stick by them. I am not talking about pushing beliefs on others as some religious and political groups do. Instead, I am referring to taking a stand on the issues of the day and not being afraid to hang in there when the going gets a little difficult. President Lincoln was a prime example of a leader who did this. Over the years he unwaveringly stood by his conviction that the Union must be preserved even if it meant civil war.

On a personal note, my strong belief in the equality of all people has led me not to join any

Keep true, never be ashamed of doing right; decide on what you think is right, and stick to it.

George Eliot

club or organization that does not openly support membership from minority groups. I also make it a point not to participate in or condone ethnic, racial, religious, and sexist jokes. *Even the hint of prejudice of any type has no place in a well-run organization.*

10. **Keep an open mind when someone questions the way you handled something or criticizes your work**. Try to view such input as information only. Do not take it personally. You are free to reject it or use it as you see fit.

> The trouble with most of us is we would rather be ruined by praise than saved by criticism.
>
> Dr. Norman Vincent Peale

No one in a leadership position is immune from criticism. In fact, the higher you go in an organization, the more you can expect. The trick is to sort out the negative feedback that is valid, which can help you improve your performance, from that which is malicious and counterproductive.

11. **Be diplomatic in resolving conflicts with others**. An occasional dispute with an associate is bound to arise. Resolving the matter with a minimum of friction depends on how skilled you are at negotiating. Avoid the tendency that some managers have to always achieve total victory. Sticking with an "all or nothing" strategy too long frequently yields nothing. Work to understand the issues behind the conflict. Look for solutions that are in the best interest of all involved.

Winning a single battle may cause you to lose the entire war. Everyone involved must benefit in some way from the resolution. Otherwise, they may become bitter and look for ways to get even in the future. It is a wise leader who sees conflict as an opportunity to improve both task accomplishment and working relationships.

When you disagree with a recommendation, never attack it head-on by saying it is wrong or ill-conceived. Instead, present a case for another approach that you believe will better serve the needs of the business.

12. **Develop a professional, energetic image.** Always dress conservatively and speak correctly. John T. Molloy, author of *Dress for Success* and *Molloy's Live for Success,* interviewed hundreds of executives to determine their views about success. Nearly everyone agreed that "a person, who dresses conservatively, speaks standard English, and carries himself in an erect manner has a better chance of succeeding than someone who does not."[4] Such habits suggest self-confidence and authority; both are important leadership traits.

    Besides maintaining a businesslike appearance, develop an energetic look. Be alert, walk purposely, and sit upright. If you look and act as if you have an important mission to fulfill, your personnel will take their own work seriously.

13. **Be a team player.** If the people who report to you see how well you cooperate and assist colleagues on your level, they will be inclined to follow suit. There is no place in an organization for the overly ambitious person who only looks out for number one.

    The best way to channel your ambition is to be ambitious—not for yourself—but for your department or organization. Put all your energies into accomplishing team goals first. After that, all the other things, like your recognition and advancement, will take care of themselves.

    Being a team player requires that you subordinate your own personal interests and ambitions to those of the organization to which you belong.

    Selfish superstars contribute little to the success of a business enterprise. For this reason they are seldom promoted to top management, or if they are

Aim for service, not success, and success will follow.
Bits & Pieces

promoted, they seldom last long. I once asked a senior officer at Kraft Foods about his secret of success. His reply: "Being helpful to my colleagues and letting them take credit for the results."

14. **Show Enthusiasm.** Every organization needs a cheerleader. People are attracted to upbeat personalities, and a leader's enthusiastic spirit brings out the same in others.

Every great and commanding moment in the annals of the world is the triumph of some enthusiasm.
Ralph Waldo Emerson

Everyone has down days from time to time. At the Mary Kay Cosmetics Company the managers are taught to "fake it until you make it," or to act enthusiastic until they feel better.

15. **Treat your employees as you would like to be treated—with respect and dignity.** In a survey, employees from various companies were asked to identify the qualities that they most wanted from their jobs. The number one response: "Co-workers who treat them with respect." [5]

A synopsis of a research study printed in the *New York Times* indicated that there is a strong correlation between a person's self-image and whether or not he or she treats others with respect and dignity. It follows then that if you as a leader can raise the self-image of your personnel, they will respond favorably to fellow employees and customers.

A great leader never sets himself above his followers except in carrying responsibilities.
James Ormont

Far too many executives give only lip service to the concept of treating all levels of employees as they would like to be treated. The widespread use of executive dining rooms, separate washrooms, and designated parking spaces only fosters a feeling of separation or estrangement between management and hourly personnel. How many managers punch a time clock when they arrive at work each morning? Very few. And yet, hourly personnel are often expected to punch-in to account for their time so they do not cheat. Treating people with respect and dignity means you cannot allow some groups in your organization to feel suspect, unappreciated, and shutout. Effective leaders demonstrate sensitivity to this issue by maintaining a low profile in their business and private affairs and by placing the welfare of their personnel above their own.

16. **Build networks by being friendly and by unselfishly helping others.** The informal network in a company is just as important as the formal network. Much of your success as a leader depends on the willingness of peers and associates to help you by providing information and by supporting your programs. During times of crisis this support becomes increasingly important. If you make a serious mistake or your results suddenly falter, you need others to rally behind you. The degree of such support depends on how well you are liked and how much you helped others in the past.

17. **Learn to keep your mouth shut.** Loose lips sink careers! Over the years I have seen many careers ruined by careless talk. As Michael Korda, Editor-In-Chief of Simon Schuster, says,

> *Learn to keep quiet and look wise— people will naturally suppose that you know more than you probably do. Don't gossip and don't talk about your plans. A reputation for keeping secrets far outweighs the easy popularity that retailing gossip may win you. The further you go in your career, the truer this is. In higher management, secrecy is golden.* [6]

Not only do loose lips sink careers, they can also cost dearly in terms of defamation lawsuits. Any disparaging remark you make concerning an employee's national origin, race, sex, or religion can be the basis of litigation against you and your company. You can even be held liable for passing on a negative rumor about a person even if you didn't originate the rumor.

18. **Avoid the ever-present danger of becoming too comfortable in your job.** This happened to Rocky Balboa in the movie *Rocky III*. With considerable wealth from product endorsements and speaking engagements, he lost the competitive edge of a hungry, up-and-coming fighter. It was only after near ruination that Rocky decided to regain "the eye of the tiger."

As a manager you're paid to be uncomfortable. If you're comfortable, it's a sure sign you're doing things wrong.
Peter Drucker

Exceptional leaders realize that when things are going well they should become concerned. At this point the natural human tendency to let down occurs. Remember that the competition is probably staying up nights trying to figure out ways of beating you. It is a highly competitive world, so keep learning, keep hustling, and keep dreaming up new and better ways of doing things.

19. **Never! Never! Never! Never give up!** Believe it or not, these six words comprised an entire speech by Winston Churchill. They say it all!

20. **Maintain a positive mental attitude.** Others like to be associated with a leader who has a positive outlook about life and who has a sense of direction. To have such attitudes, you must first believe in yourself and your ability to win . . . to visualize success at all times . . . to think of yourself as a champion. Dr. Norman Vincent Peale called this "positive imaging." He once told me that the key to success is: "Holding in your conscious mind what you want to achieve and then striving in everything you do to make the image reality." William James, the noted psychologist, said, "The greatest discovery of my generation is that man can alter his

Success is a mind game.
Tag Heuer Advertisement

lifestyle simply by altering his attitude of mind." Walt Disney put it another way, "If you can dream it, you can do it." People can accomplish almost anything in life if they believe strongly enough that they can do it.

Many athletes and entertainers mentally prepare before they perform. To do so they generally use a three-step approach. First, they get themselves into a totally relaxed state. Second, they picture the physical surroundings where they will perform. Finally, they visualize each step of their performance.

This imaging approach also works in business when you have to perform under pressure. Before I give a major speech, I create a visual image of the meeting room, the podium, and the audience. I then think about the key message I want to get across and the specific points that will enhance the message. Finally, I anticipate the types of questions that might be asked and what responses I will make. This focused imaging creates a tremendous feeling of confidence and being in control of the situation.

Having a positive mental attitude is of particular importance if you have suffered a serious setback at work, such as being demoted or losing your job. You can have all the ability and drive in the world, but if you do not believe you can overcome failure, you have little chance of making a comeback.

Just as success comes to those who constantly hold positive mental images in their minds, failure comes to those who are preoccupied with negative thoughts. The latter has become known as the "Wallenda Factor." In 1978, while traversing a high wire in downtown San Juan, Puerto Rico, the famous aerialist Karl Wallenda fell to his death. Later his wife told reporters that her husband was

When the imagination and the willpower are harmoniously pulling in the same direction, an irresistible force is the result.

Emile Couèe

What you hold in your imagination about yourself, you will become.

Nothing can stop the man with the right mental attitude from achieving his goal; nothing on earth can help the man with the wrong mental attitude.

W. W. Ziege

The remarkable thing is we have a choice every day regarding the attitude we embrace for that day.

Charles Swindle

obsessed with the feeling that he would fall. "All Karl thought about for three straight months prior to it was falling."[7] He was so concerned about his safety that he personally supervised the installation of the tightrope—something he had never done before.[8] By focusing on the negative, Wallenda lost his concentration and made a fatal mistake.

How does one go about the task of overcoming negative thinking? I have found that the best approach is to train yourself to recognize each negative thought that enters your mind. Then immediately replace the negative thought with a positive one on the same subject. For example, if you find yourself dwelling on how impossible it is to achieve a revenue or cost target because you do not have the necessary resources to do so, **stop** and say to yourself: "That's negative thinking." Then immediately begin to consider how to accomplish the mission in other ways, such as by redirecting present resources and by establishing different priorities. Another example: The next time you catch yourself complaining about traveling so much, recognize your negative thoughts and then begin considering how valuable the trips are in broadening your horizons and in learning firsthand about what needs to be done to improve the performance of your operation.

In summary, your subordinates and peers "know you like a book." Your likes, dislikes, feelings, beliefs, and attitudes become common knowledge. How your employees perceive you as a person will determine if they like you, respect you, or just tolerate you. The type of example you set goes a long way toward determining which viewpoint they will adopt.

Before you go on to the next chapter I'd like to leave you with a very important point about leading by example. And that is: **Everything you do as a leader** must be based on high ideals and values. For in the end, your character is what is enduring in life.

7

The Effective Leader Holds Subordinates Accountable

In chapter 4, I discussed how a leader could coach employees into improving their performance. Yet coaching alone will not always work. An effective leader encourages employees, but also holds them accountable.

Most people are accustomed to being held accountable for their actions and the consequences of **their** failures. Leaders, on the other hand, are held accountable for **both** their own actions and those of their personnel. Leaders must be able to accept criticism when their people make mistakes even though they, as leaders, were not directly involved in causing the failures. Once you accept this philosophy, you are on your way to becoming an effective leader.

An effective leader is tough-minded when it comes to obtaining results from team members. After clear, measurable expectations have been communicated, excuses cannot be tolerated when achievable goals are not met. **What counts are the results, not that the person really tried.** If an employee does not measure up after retraining and repeated warnings, the leader must have the fortitude to take appropriate disciplinary action.

It's important to understand the full meaning of the word discipline. It means "corrective teaching", as well as the more common meaning of punishment. The approach recommended in this chapter combine cer-

Anybody who accepts mediocrity in school, on the job, in life, is a person who compromises; and when the leader compromises, the whole organization compromises.
Charles F. Knight, Chairman, Emerson Electric Company

tain facets of coaching with traditional disciplinary approaches. When deficiencies are first spotted, you must find out who is responsible and hold them accountable. If you ignore substandard work, it becomes the norm.

Before you call an employee in to discuss a performance concern that has not been corrected by coaching, be sure to get all the facts about the problem. Inexperienced managers often jump to conclusions based on incomplete information. There are always two sides to a story, so never accuse or blame a person until you have heard his or her side.

If after securing the facts and listening to the employee you are still displeased, you need to let him know how you feel. If you are angry, upset, or frustrated, let it be known. Look the individual straight in the eye and say, "I have given you about as much latitude as possible, and now it is up to you to take the necessary corrective action." Just telling the offender to fix the problem is insufficient. The person may need further advice on how to do so. There should be a clear understanding of what will happen next if the desired results are not obtained.

During such accountability sessions I find it useful to let the person know that I really want him to succeed and that I will go out of my way to provide the necessary support and assistance to do so. Also, I always make it a point to close the meeting with some words of hope and encouragement, such as, "I know you're capable of doing better," or "I am confident you can correct the problem." For the individual to make the effort to change and improve, he must believe that all is not lost and that you will keep an open mind about the future.

Sometimes the counseling approach does not work and stronger action is necessary. It may be appropriate to write a letter of concern or warning. Such

Permissiveness is neglect of duty.
Zig Ziglar

An effective leader is able to deal with occasionally being unpopular or even disliked by some people.

letters should detail performance deficiencies and outline the expected results during the next three to six months. With such letters it is a good idea to include the ways that you intend to help the employee improve. Once again, it is important that the offender realize that there is still hope that he can regain good standing. The best way to get that message across is to say that you will remove the letter of concern from his file in six months if there is substantial performance improvement. Make it clear in the letter that "continued substandard results will cause further disciplinary action up to and including termination." **Never send or give such a letter to someone without first discussing it in person.**

After giving a written reprimand, you can expect the offender to be upset and unhappy with you. He may launch a campaign to discredit you with other employees or even your superiors. At this point you need to have the courage to take some heat. Stand firm. Others will soon realize that you acted fairly and had the best interests of the organization at heart.

In every organization there are some people (sometimes as high as 10 percent) who will not respond to anything you do. They just don't care!

If the warning letter does not stimulate improvement, the next step should be to give the individual time off **without** pay. Normally, a day or two is sufficient to demonstrate the seriousness of the problem. It has been my experience that this strong demonstration of resolve to reject substandard performance works in some cases and not in others. Some employees will return from their days off with an entirely new attitude and a strong determination to improve. Others will harbor deep-seated animosity and will look for ways to get even with you or the company.

If time off does not work, termination is usually necessary. Still, possibly one final action can be taken to stimulate the individual to change. Sometimes an unorthodox approach will get results when everything else fails. One idea is to give the offender a day off

with pay for him to think about the seriousness of the performance problem and to develop a written correction plan. Some people respond favorably to this last chance gesture by returning to work with renewed dedication. If the plan is not followed, the individual has no one to blame but himself.

On other occasions, you may have to try a more direct approach. When I was a manager for Sealtest Foods, I employed a route deliveryman named Joe who had the habit of abusing overtime. When it was apparent that his workweek would run over forty hours, he did everything possible to stretch out the remaining hours and thus maximize his overtime pay. I "coached" him, but he ignored my efforts. Finally, I told Joe that I would ride with him for several days to do a comprehensive time and motion study. After the second day, it was obvious to both of us that the route could easily be covered within a normal forty-hour week. I then prepared a report of my findings and requested a meeting with Joe and my boss. When Joe realized that I intended to pursue the matter aggressively, he admitted he was wrong and indicated that he would shape-up in the future.

Before terminating an employee, you might also consider reassigning him. Perhaps another job will be more suited to his abilities. Too often, talented employees are misplaced in jobs that are unchallenging or too demanding. They may prefer a job more suited to their talents, even if it is a demotion.

Always consider what is best for the organization when making difficult personnel decisions.

After exhausting all corrective means without results, the only alternative left is to let the employee go. Since this is a drastic step, accomplish it with sensitivity and care. A former boss once gave me this advice: "I know it's difficult to terminate someone, but there eventually comes a point when the welfare of the entire group suffers if the rotten apple is allowed to remain in the barrel." Remembering this comment has helped me sleep nights when confronted with the difficult job of disciplining nonperformers.

I need to make several points about holding people accountable by administering an escalating form of discipline: first, a serious problem exists with the leader if he has to frequently discipline employees. If this occurs, the leader has probably failed to earn the respect and loyalty of his people. An effective leader seldom has to use his power, but the employees know he will do so if necessary. Second, being too aggressive in the pursuit of results may alienate employees to the point that they eventually revolt. The revolt usually starts with passive resistance to directives and then escalates with complaint letters being sent to top management. Eventually the word gets out that the leader has no following. Leadership changes must then be made.

Leading is like holding a dove ... squeeze too tight, you kill it. Open your hand too much, you let it go.
Tommy Lasorda

The best advice, therefore, is to go slow in introducing the philosophy of accountability in your organization. Prior to doing so you must build a coalition of base support by gaining the trust and loyalty of key personnel. Then involve everyone in the process of making needed changes. **Finally, step back and let your people do their jobs with minimal interference.** If you follow this advice, you will seldom have to apply escalating levels of discipline.

8

The Effective Leader Has Courage

Courage is the intangible leadership quality of which greatness is made. It is demonstrated when a person endures severe pressure, conflict, or adversity with grace and dignity. All exceptional leaders seem to have their fair share of it.

How does someone acquire courage? There is no simple formula for doing so. Nevertheless, I have come to the conclusion that an individual's continued courage under trying circumstances comes from spiritual strength. As Cicero said, "A man of courage is also full of faith." Those who believe in God or something more powerful than themselves are better able to face adversity straight on and inspire others by doing so.

Outstanding leaders "plug-in" to power sources external to themselves.

Let us look at some of the ways leaders demonstrate courage. First, they are willing to "stand up and be counted" for what they believe in. Courageous leaders do not suffer from the crippling need to be loved by everyone. For example, they are not afraid to say "no" to unreasonable requests and demands placed on them and to take strong positions on issues of importance. When such issues arise, courageous leaders do not remain on the sidelines by keeping quiet. Instead, they strongly express their opinions. Though they may be ridiculed and disliked from time to time, they continue to stand up for their beliefs.

A willingness to put oneself on the line is a very important element of leadership.
Lee Iacocca

Second, leaders have the courage to pick themselves up after defeat and work even harder than

81

before. Successfully leading an organization every day is a tough game. You do not always meet your objectives. Occasionally you will get in hot water with others. Even leaders with a high batting average are going to strike out periodically.

General George Washington, for example, made a series of initial mistakes in conducting the Revolutionary War against the British. At one point it was thought that the war would be lost. Yet Washington learned from his errors, adopted new strategies, and eventually prevailed. When Lee Iacocca was fired by Henry Ford II in 1978, he could have retired to a life of luxury. Instead, he decided to keep going by taking the ailing Chrysler Corporation from near bankruptcy to prosperity.

I have never known a successful business leader who did not have at least one incident of serious failure in his or her career. Good leaders have the courage to take risks, to face failure, and to learn from each mistake. When failure is viewed from this perspective, it becomes a stepping stone to the future.

People generally do not learn much from their successes; they learn more from their mistakes. They gain new insights and perspectives about themselves by reflecting on what they did wrong and how they can do better in the future.

Third, leaders have the courage to face inevitable conflict openly and head on. Whenever strong-willed people interact on a frequent basis, there will be occasional disagreements and conflict. The effective leader recognizes that this is a fact of life and does not shy away from conflict because of the tension and stress involved.

Possibly no president was more criticized and slandered than Abraham Lincoln as he focused on preserving the nation during the dark days of 1861-63. With the rising death toll, Lincoln came under severe

One of the secrets of success is to refuse to let temporary setbacks defeat you.

Mary Kay Ash

Future triumphs are often born from past mistakes.

pressure to negotiate a compromise treaty with the Confederacy. Criticism came from everywhere—families of slain soldiers, peace organizers, Congress, Lincoln's party, and even his own cabinet. What hurt Lincoln the most were the attacks on his character by people he thought were his friends. With exceptional courage, Lincoln persevered by holding firm to his belief that in the end his course would be vindicated.[1]

In 1946, Branch Rickey, President and General Manager of the Brooklyn Dodgers, decided to face inevitable conflict by doing what was right—integrating major league sports. The signing of Jackie Robinson to a Dodger contract sent shock waves through the baseball world. At first, some of the Dodgers refused to play with Robinson. There was a threat of strikes by the Cardinals, Cubs, and Phillies. Hate mail was abundant, and some of Rickey's colleagues would not speak to him. Amidst all this ridicule and conflict, Branch Rickey never wavered from his deep-rooted belief in equal opportunity for all people and in his personal support for Jackie Robinson.[2]

Branch Rickey's courage was more than equaled by that of Jackie Robinson, who endured the constant insults of bigoted players and fans alike. He fought back not with anger and fists but with superior performance at bat, on the bases, and in the field. On the fiftieth anniversary of his major league debut on April 15, 1947, a *USA Today* editorial read: "On that historic day Jackie Robinson broke the color line in baseball and changed both sports and America forever. . . . He and the black athletes who followed him did more to shift the way we think about race than all the preachers, pundits, marchers, and politicians."[3]

Occasionally, some conflict is necessary in an organization to get things moving—to obtain action where there are bureaucratic roadblocks or procrastination. In explaining this principle to my people I use an analogy: "A little friction is often needed to get traction." The trick is to keep the conflict controlled so as not to create warring factions that undermine co-operation.

Fourth, leaders have the courage and strength to bear their burdens. The best example of courage that I have ever witnessed was that demonstrated by Don Harrison, my father-in-law, as he fought his battle with terminal cancer. Never once during his long illness did I ever hear him complain. He was always positive and thinking of others to the very end. He was an inspiration to everyone who knew him.

The measure of a man is the way he bears up under misfortune.
Plutarch

In the spring of 1995, Christopher Reeve, who starred in the role of Superman, had a tragic fall from a horse. The fall injured his spinal cord, leaving him totally paralyzed from the neck down. Instead of wallowing in self-pity, Reeve had the courage to refocus his life on what he **could** do rather than what he couldn't. He dedicated his new life to helping others in similar conditions by raising money for medical research. Reeve's dream: "That others will not suffer what he has had to endure."

Finally, leaders have the courage to adapt and change as conditions and situations merit. This is not an easy task for leaders who have been successful over the years by doing things their own way. The reasoning of such people goes something like this: "Why change? I've been successful in the past."

Courage is an opportunity that sooner or later is presented to all of us.
John F. Kennedy

Still, as everyone knows, success is fleeting in our rapidly changing business environment. What was appropriate a few years ago may not work today. Just look what happened to the International Harvester Company and Eastern Airlines. Years ago, Wall Street considered these firms the leaders in their industries. Unable to change with the times, Harvester is no longer in the farm equipment business and Eastern has been liquidated.

When you're through changing, you're through.
Bruce Barton

There is another reason why people fail to adapt and change: most of us prefer the established routine. We are all creatures of comfort. We like the familiar because we can count on it. Surprises are uncomfortable, and change creates uncertainty. This leads to tension and stress.

Outstanding leaders "embrace" the uncertainty that is caused by change. They're not afraid of the unknown; rather they welcome it as a means of fostering their own growth and development. Deepak Chopra says, "Openness for change creates the potential for infinite possibilities to occur." Faced with an uncertain future, the natural human reaction to change is to become preoccupied with negative thoughts. Constant worry dissipates our mental and physical energy to the point that we lose our creativity. On the other hand, when we condition ourselves to accept that change is inevitable, we can focus all our energy on figuring out ways to shape the future for the benefit of the organization and ourselves.

We cannot direct the wind ... but we can adjust the sails.
Author Unknown

In this chapter, leadership courage was identified as a person's perseverance and determination when faced with adversity or an unusual challenge. Such courage is demonstrated in many ways, such as:

- being able to say "no" and take strong positions on important issues,
- responding to defeat by trying even harder,
- facing conflict openly and head on,
- bearing one's burdens, and
- embracing change.

9

The Effective Leader Shows Confidence in People

Few things help an individual more than to place responsibility upon him, and to let him know you trust him.

Booker T. Washington,
Up from Slavery

One of the biggest mistakes leaders make is to undersell their people by not having faith in them. Years ago I learned a valuable lesson about leadership while working for Frank Borman, the president of Eastern Airlines. Borman had asked me to design some slides that he needed for a corporate management conference in San Juan. A week later we reviewed the finished slides with the Graphics/Photography Department employees who were to operate the projectors at the conference. After seeing the slides, I suggested that an extra set be prepared for me to carry to the conference, just in case the originals were lost. Borman's response was quick and strong: "We don't need an extra set! I have full confidence that these people will not lose the slides and will do an excellent job with the presentation." You can imagine how I felt. It bothered me a great deal until I realized I had learned an important leadership principle.

It's trust in people that makes them rise to the occasion.

Stephen Covey

You must trust your people even if it involves some risk. Obviously, there will be situations in which you will have to withhold trust by checking on others, but for most business matters it is wise to have faith that your personnel will do their jobs in a competent manner. **Having trust in people builds their confidence and stimulates them to do their best.**

10

The Effective Leader Is Decisive

Successful leaders have the courage to take action where others hesitate.

Decision-making is a basic ingredient of leadership. It is not important whether the leader actually comes up with the proposed actions or simply endorses them. The key is that the leader does act decisively. He or she overcomes the fear of failing or being second-guessed. A leader gathers as many facts as possible, consults with others, and then decides on a course of action. Gerald Greenwald, CEO of United Airlines, is a strong advocate of not wasting time in decision making. He says, "It's better to make decisions quickly and be right eight out of ten times and scramble to fix the other two, than taking the time to be right every time."[1]

Once the decision is made, the effective leader does not waste time on second thoughts. The thrust of such a person is always forward—looking for the next challenge, focusing on the next decision.

Your decisions will always be better if you do what is right for the organization, not what is right for yourself.

Every effective leader occasionally makes a poor decision. When this occurs, what counts is how the leader handles the situation. Those who willingly admit their mistakes and take corrective action will usually be forgiven by the organization. Most people do not expect their leaders to be perfect. They are willing to accept some errors as long as the leader holds to the principle of trying to do what is right for the organization as a whole. What they do resent, however, is a leader who reverses a decision when pressured by a few vocal individuals or a special interest group.

In today's work environment it is imperative that team members be **involved**, one way or another, in the decision-making process. People in the workforce are better educated and more self-directed today. They do not expect to make all of the decisions themselves, but at a minimum they want to be consulted and be able to fully express their thoughts and ideas **before** important actions are taken.

Why is it so important to involve your personnel in decision making? The obvious reason, of course, is that better decisions are possible when different opinions and ideas are considered. More importantly, people carry out decisions that they have participated in making much more enthusiastically than they carry out orders from the boss. It has been proven over and over again that **involvement leads to commitment.**

In involving team members in the decision making process, the leader should provide clear definition of who will make the final decisions under various circumstances. In some cases the leader will delegate decisions to the team and in other cases, the team's role will be to collect and analyze pertinent data so the leader can decide.

Most effective leaders entrust able members of their department with the responsibility of deciding most matters within the confines of their annual business plans. Such leaders facilitate and guide this process to ensure that decisions are timely and do not adversely affect other work groups. In effect, they function as an advisor or consultant.

Normally, I use this approach by asking team members to study a problem and then take appropriate action. The results have been excellent, not only in the quality of decisions, but also in developing people to be resourceful and responsible. However, I do not permit such latitude when the issue is controversial between different divisions or departments or when the decision requires significant unplanned expenditures. Under such circumstances I always seek the

The very essence of all power to influence lies in getting the other person to participate.

Harry A. Overstreet

opinions and advice of those who will be impacted by the decisions and then make the decision myself. I try to give everyone a chance to be heard, to agree or disagree as they see fit. At times I deliberately encourage debate by taking opposing positions to the majority viewpoints or by asking another staff member to do so. I have found that open, spirited discussion creates a sense of satisfaction and commitment to the decisions that are eventually made. After hearing all sides and asking numerous questions, I either make the decision on the spot or set a final date for doing so. This way everyone knows that action will be taken.

Obviously, you cannot please everyone with your decisions, nor should you try. **The important thing, once again, is that your personnel have input about major issues that impact them**. After that, I believe the leader must make the tough calls by saying, "This is what we'll do."

In making the tough calls I have always found it helpful to ask myself, "What's the worst thing that could happen as the result of making a poor decision, and can the organization recover?" Realizing that you **can** bounce back helps overcome the natural fear of failure that comes from making difficult choices. Asking, "What's the best thing that could happen as a result of this decision?" often leads the organization to new heights, and at least focuses energy toward the right goals.

In the final analysis, the decision-making burden belongs to the leader.

11

The Effective Leader Has a Strong Sense of Urgency

A trait I look for in everyone I hire is a strong sense of urgency, for without it progress is slow. The attitude has to be, "Let's do it, and let's do it **now**!"

In their best-selling book, *In Search of Excellence,* Thomas Peters and Robert Waterman identify eight attributes that great companies have in common. One of the most important attributes is a "bias for action."[1] In other words, the best companies are led by executives who constantly stimulate action to make things happen. These executives just don't sit around discussing ideas endlessly and waiting for the right time to implement them. Instead, they ensure that a reasonable level of planning is done and then they act—even if the timing is not quite right.

When I was a management trainee for Sealtest Foods, I learned a valuable lesson about the need to take corrective action quickly. The plant where I worked had a street entrance where large milk tankers came in to off-load. Prior to entering the plant, the trucks had to drive across a wide pedestrian sidewalk. In my opinion this was an accident waiting to happen. Surely, it would not be long until an unsuspecting person was caught under those rear wheels. On numerous occasions I brought this to the attention of the plant manager. Nothing was done until **after** there was a serious accident. At the time I can remember saying to myself, "When I'm in charge, I'll never let this kind of thing happen. Never!"

The right man is the one who seizes the moment.

Goethe

90

Contrast this lack of urgency with what happened years later when I was visiting the Federal Express station in Akron, Ohio. While in the office I noticed a computer message indicating that the Cleveland station, some seventy miles away, had received by mistake several perishable packages for a customer in Akron. Because it was Friday, I was concerned that the perishables would spoil if rerouted back through the hub in Memphis for Monday delivery. I called the Cleveland station manager to ask him what he intended to do. His response: "I'm already working on a way to get them to the customer today." This is the attitude of a winner!

One of the most difficult challenges of leadership is to maintain a high degree of urgency to accomplish difficult goals year after year. I have always believed it is easier to build a winning team from scratch than to keep it continuously on top. With repeated success people tend to get complacent.

One way for a leader to avoid this problem is to periodically freshen the organization by changing team members' roles and responsibilities. Sometimes partial or total reorganization is necessary. At other times new "blood" needs to be brought into the organization. The trick is to maintain a balance between organization stability and the feeling of excitement and commitment that comes from periodically taking on new challenges.

A major reorganization should not occur more frequently than every two or three years. More frequent changes create high levels of insecurity. Organizational fine-tuning and minor adjustments, however, should occur as needed.

Another way to overcome complacency in a work group and to rekindle a sense of urgency is to take some unusual or unexpected action. In the late 1940's, the Eastern Airlines baggage-mishandling rate

Even though you are on the right track, you'll get run over if you just sit there.
Will Rogers

had deteriorated to an unsatisfactory level. Passenger complaints were steadily increasing. Captain Eddie Rickenbacker, Eastern's chairman, was furious. When his usual exhortations to his officers failed to have an impact, he decided to take the situation into his own hands by calling a special meeting of management personnel in Miami. It was summer in Miami, and the weather was hot and humid. In those days air conditioning was not available. As the out-of-town managers checked into the hotel, they were told that their bags would be placed in their rooms. Instead, Rickenbacker had the bags locked up in a storage area overnight.

In his autobiography Rickenbacker tells what happened next:

> There they were for the meeting the next morning, unshaven, teeth unbrushed, wearing dirty shirts. There was no sign of the baggage all day. That night it was delivered, with a great pounding on all the doors, at 3:00 a.m. At the opening session the second morning, I said, "Now you know how the customer feels when you mishandle his luggage."[2]

Occasionally, it's necessary for the leader to be unpredictable and inconsistent. If you are too predictable, some people will take advantage of you.

When I was the Newark Airport station manager for Eastern Airlines, I did something similar but less dramatic to overcome management complacency. At the time we were experiencing a rash of accidents due to operator carelessness. Too many airplanes were being damaged on the ramp. It was apparent that the managers were not holding the ramp equipment operators accountable. The problem continued even after the managers were directed several times to take corrective action.

One Sunday evening I received a call from the Control Center manager, Dominick Zappia, informing me of another serious incidence of damage to an aircraft. This was the last straw! I told Dominick to call all the managers, even those at home, to tell them to report to a special meeting at 10:00 p.m. that night, even though it was Sunday, to resolve the problem once and for all. We talked into the early morning until everyone was satisfied that we had an action plan that would work.

Good leaders seldom need to take such dramatic action to get results. Their personnel will normally correct problems when asked to do so. It is only when everything else fails that the leader should look for an unorthodox way to inspire action.

Finally, organizational complacency is avoidable if leaders maintain their own sense of urgency. It is imperative that they never let down because as soon as they do, others will quickly follow suit. Richard Sloma in *No-Nonsense Management* says, **"If the captain relaxes too long, the crew will go on vacation."**

Leaders, like everyone else, often suffer from the human tendency to let up or coast once they've achieved success. After the initial excitement of striving against strong odds and prevailing, it's difficult to continue to operate with intensity. The best approach for avoiding this lack of forward movement is to set new goals for yourself and your organization.

There are a number of other things leaders can do to keep up their own motivation and enthusiasm. One approach is to vary your leadership focus and style periodically. Too many major changes can be confusing and threatening to subordinates, but leaders should add variety when necessary to keep the work stimulating and interesting.

No one keeps up his enthusiasm automatically. Enthusiasm must be nourished with new actions, new aspirations, new efforts, and new vision. It is one's own fault if his enthusiasm is gone; he has failed to feed it.

Papyrus

Strong leaders have a relentless discomfort with the status quo.

Periodically take a little risk by developing and implementing an innovative operational approach that has the potential for a high payoff. Establish goals for your department that are more challenging than those previously established. Periodically change the location and agenda format of your department meetings. Start coming to work earlier than usual and leaving a little earlier. Give assignments to staff members that you normally handle.

Another approach to perk up your enthusiasm is to become an expert in a function you know little about, but think you might enjoy. Pick an area of interest related to your present job. For example, if you are a sales manager, become knowledgeable about sales training or marketing. Likewise, if your firm is expanding overseas, learn about foreign cultures. In time you will be recognized for your new expertise. Others will seek your advice, which could lead to a promotion or even an entirely new career.

The idea is to try new approaches to avoid getting into the comfortable rut of doing the same thing over and over again. You will feel better about your job, and others will note your positive attitude.

Of all the things a leader should fear, complacency heads the list. To remind me of what can happen to an organization that has lost its will to win, I keep a snapshot of one of our competitor's pickup and delivery trucks parked in front of an office building with the driver sound asleep. He should have been utilizing his spare time doing paperwork or canvassing a building for new customers.

The role of the leader is to keep everyone energized and inspired by (1) periodically changing or rotating team member responsibilities, (2) taking unusual or unexpected action, and (3) setting the example of urgency for others to follow.

12

The Effective Leader Makes Every Minute Count

Take a moment to answer the following questions:

- Do you take work home on a regular basis to keep up?
- Do you keep deferring important projects because of insufficient time to concentrate on them?
- Does excessive paperwork or E-mail messages regularly pile up?

Time is your most valuable personal resource. Use it wisely because it can't be replaced.

A "yes" answer to these questions means that you are not running the job; the job is running you. Buried in detail and lacking focus, you are neglecting the critical leadership dimension of visualizing the future and preparing for it. Instead, you constantly seem to be in a reactive or "fire fighting" mode. The paperwork continues to stack up, putting you further and further behind. It is a never ending and self-defeating cycle caused by the poor management of time.

Thankfully there is a way out of this predicament. Time management skills can be developed and perfected, leading to substantial improvement in your productivity.

This chapter is devoted to the presentation of techniques used by successful leaders to make the best use of their most precious commodity—time.

Choosing and performing activities with high leverage is the key to managerial effectiveness.[1]
   Andrew S. Grove,
   President, Intel
   Corporation

1. **Identify the areas of your job with the greatest payoff for your organization**. In our fast-paced business world there are often more tasks to be performed than can be accomplished. The trick is to identify the few activities that are critical to overall success. If these functions progress well, overall success is virtually assured. Some people call this the 80/20 rule—80 percent of the performance results come from focusing on 20 percent of the job. For a service manager the 20 percent involves selecting quality service representatives and training them extensively. For a production manager it is ensuring that a strong quality ethic exists among all employees. Job functions that have the greatest payoff are called critical success areas.

2. **Develop goals for each critical success area.** These goals can be for yourself or your organization. To be meaningful, they must be: (a) challenging, (b) understandable, (c) obtainable, (d) measurable.

   Most managers readily accomplish the task of making goals challenging and understandable. Difficulties arise when teams are forced to stretch too much in performance. With intense global competition and the desire to constantly improve earnings, the operating manager is under extreme pressure to maximize short-term profits by accepting ambitious, often unrealistic, productivity and cost objectives. This places him in an untenable position. It can be a no-win situation. If the manager resists the goals too vigorously, he risks being branded as timid or ineffectual. At the same time, if he accepts unrealistic goals and fails, he may lose bonus opportunities or even lose his job. Placed in such a pressure cooker, it is no wonder that some managers seek relief by compromising their standards of honesty and integrity.

Disciplined focus is what distinguishes those who make things happen from those that watch things happen.

The only way out of this predicament is for top management to ensure that goals are challenging, understandable, **and obtainable**. This must be done even at the expense of short-term earnings.

3. **Set weekly priorities to facilitate the accomplishment of goals.** Each Friday evening before I leave work for the weekend, I spend time thinking about what I want to accomplish the next week. The tasks that relate to my goals I give top ranking. These are the "must complete" items. Everything else is labeled "do when possible." Other leaders do their weekly planning Sunday evening or when they first arrive at the office Monday morning. The idea is to utilize the approach with which you are most comfortable.

Nothing is as necessary for success as the single-minded pursuit of an objective.
    Frederick W. Smith,
        Chairman,
    Federal Express
        Corporation

The best way to insure focus on your weekly priorities is to support them with daily plans. Before arriving at the office each morning, take a few minutes to visualize what you want to accomplish during the day. Make a list and check off each item as it is accomplished. Doing so will give you a strong sense of accomplishment.

4. **Do the most important things first and never waste time on unimportant activities.** This sounds simple, but it is not. People tend to gravitate toward tasks that are enjoyable and avoid the difficult or disagreeable ones. Unfortunately, successful performance always entails doing some tasks you might not enjoy. The best approach is to force yourself to do these tasks first. Stick with them until they are completed and then reward yourself by tackling something more pleasurable.

The art of becoming wise is the art of knowing what to look over.
    Wm. James

The best way to separate the "wheat from the chaff" is to constantly ask yourself, "Does it really matter if I do this task or not?" And if it does matter, "Does it have to be done now or can it be postponed?"

5. **Concentrate on a few things at a time.** Leaders need to realize that they can only bring their special

abilities to bear on a few critical success areas at one time. Therefore, focus on one or two areas that will benefit most from your leadership expertise. Stick with them until you are satisfied with the results. Then you are ready to move on to another challenge.

The amount of time you spend on a problem or a project is not what counts; rather, it is the amount of uninterrupted time. To illustrate the value of this concept, let us apply it to the problem of developing a new program to improve customer service. The way to accomplish this task efficiently is to concentrate on it without frequent interruptions.

If you cannot obtain privacy in your own office during normal hours, seek a location where you can. I find it helpful to occasionally use a vacant office or a conference room, or any location where I can concentrate without interruptions.

I also try not to schedule or attend meetings early in the morning. I call this time period "my private time." It is routinely utilized to go over the mail, plan for the future and think creatively. This is the only part of the day that I try to control rigidly. The remainder of the day is kept open so that I am available for meetings and informal discussion with colleagues.

The number one time waster of executives—interruptions.[2]

The "morning private time" approach has a number of benefits. First, it enables me to accomplish a great deal in a minimal amount of time. Projects that used to take days are accomplished in a few hours. Second, by reviewing the mail first, I am on top of what is going on and what is on other people's minds. This prepares me to deal with important issues during the remainder of the day.

6. **Establish deadlines for yourself.** Most people work better under a little pressure. A self-imposed deadline can provide the incentive you need to keep going at full speed. I use this technique when preparing a speech. My goal is to write a rough draft two weeks in

advance of the speech. This provides ample time to improve the content and mentally rehearse the delivery.

7. **Don't be a slave to your mail.** Unattended or partially attended mail can be very distracting and can even create stress. The best way to keep this from happening is to discipline yourself to handle mail promptly and decisively. Establish a routine for processing it early in the day. Review the high priority messages and reports first, and then **take action on each item** such as deleting it, filing it, or sending it to someone else. Try not to read a report or message and then hold it for later handling. Such procrastination results in cluttered files requiring further action.

8. **Set aside a few minutes each day to think about creative ways to improve the performance of your organization.** This may be the most valuable time you ever spend! It only takes an occasional creative idea to ensure the future of your department and your career.

Performance break-throughs come from pondering the un-thinkable.

People are most creative when they are rested and away from the daily demands of the workplace. This is why you hear about the brainstorms that occur while jogging, showering in the morning, or driving to work. These are excellent times to let your mind ponder what could be achieved if there were no operational or financial constraints. Think of the ideal or ultimate way to accomplish your goals. Later on you can always make this vision more practical.

Earlier in the book an effective leader was described as someone who has a vision of what is necessary for the success of an organization and who has the ability to inspire and energize others to reach that vision. In the former area many leaders fall short. They do not spend enough time reflecting on where to take their business units in the future.

9. **Make your meetings productive.** It is estimated that more than one-half of the meetings conducted in business are unnecessary. Therefore, try to be selective in the meetings that you attend. Try to limit your participation to meetings that will enhance the results of your operation.

If you chair a meeting, keep it brief and focused. Make sure that the purpose of the meeting is clearly defined before initiating lengthy discussion. One approach for doing so is to list the objective(s) of the meeting on a flip chart and refer to it if the discussion wanders. Having agendas prepared and distributed in advance can also enhance meeting focus.

Always convey the attitude that you are primarily interested in finding solutions— not in laying blame.

Leaders can effectively utilize meetings to improve operating performance. To secure the best results from such meetings try the "no fault" approach. Prior to initiating discussion, announce the ground rule that no one is permitted to place blame on someone else or another department. Then make it clear that the only discussion allowed will be on identifying what areas need to be improved, reviewing the "root" cause(s) of substandard performance, and making suggestions for improvement.

The "no fault" meeting approach has worked well at Purolator Courier to improve the quality of delivery service. Each morning at 9:00 a.m., we conduct a systemwide telephone conference call with the district managers to review the previous day's operations. Realizing that no one will be "dressed down" by senior management for poor performance, the participants tend to be open about their problems and what they are trying to accomplish. Continued substandard performance issues are handled "off line" by the managers' immediate superiors.

10. **Maintain a balance between an open and closed-door policy.** The strategy of always keeping an open door may not be realistic anymore. The trend toward

flatter organizations and broader spans of control is placing more and more demands on the leader's time. It is therefore appropriate for the leader to occasionally close his door to concentrate on preparing a report or to complete an important project. Leaders also need thinking time in uninterrupted blocks to respond to changes, create new approaches, and revise strategies.

You cannot always afford to be interrupted by associates who "only want a minute of your time." On the other hand, you **do** want co-workers to feel free to interrupt you from time to time. As Stephanie Winston, author of *The Organized Executive,* says, "When people interrupt, realize that they come carrying gifts—information, ties of loyalty and mutual well-being. So think of the interweaving of contacts as the other part of your work."

Successful leaders utilize time differently than the average person.

Keeping a balance between an open-door and a closed-door policy requires that you make judgments concerning when to freely share your time with others and when to conserve time. Here are a few suggestions for conserving time by minimizing unwelcome interruptions without inhibiting valuable input and dialogue with associates.

a) Remain standing when unexpected visitors or colleagues "pop" into your office to engage in small talk. Unless you have time, do not invite them to sit and become comfortable. People get down to business quicker when they are on their feet.

b) Be honest with people when you cannot spend time with them. Indicate you are very busy but would be glad to meet at another time when you can devote full attention to them.

c) Minimize the need for staff members to interrupt you by periodically walking around the office. By visiting with associates in their work areas, you can satisfy their need for frequent dialogue with you plus better control the time involved.

11. **Delegate.** Continually seek ways to give your personnel more responsibility. Do not be afraid to delegate meaningful assignments. Most people have the capacity to handle additional work, especially if it provides opportunities to prove that they are capable of more demanding jobs.

Get into the habit of asking yourself if what you're doing can be handled by someone else.

Besides helping others to develop, delegation is the key to the leader's sanity. You cannot do everything yourself. The more you try, the greater the pressure and tension. Extensive delegation also frees valuable time for you to concentrate on strategic thinking.

There is more to delegating than meets the eye. It is insufficient to merely make assignments and wait for results. Adherence to the following rules of effective delegation will improve your performance in this important leadership function.

a) **Establish a climate that facilitates delegation.** There are two critical requirements necessary to do so. The first is **mutual trust.** You must trust that your people will take their assignments seriously and do the best job possible. On the other hand, they must trust that you will give them the credit for the good results they achieve. If you have the habit of stealing the credit for yourself, do not expect excellence from your personnel.

Allow your people to put their personal stamp on projects delegated to them.

The second requirement is **support**. Your people cannot be effective in their work unless they have a clear understanding of the nature of each assignment and your expectations for results. They need to know up front what they are "shooting" for in terms of the target or goal. In addition, ensure that your personnel have all the pertinent data and background information necessary to do their jobs properly. You can be helpful in this area. Distribute copies of appropriate memoranda and reports. Spend the necessary time with your staff discussing the background and ramifications of assignments. Take them to upper-level meetings where they can gain perspective of broad corporate strategy. Your efforts to share all available information and make your people feel like insiders will create commitment to the assigned projects.

The idea is to stay involved in the delegation process. Do everything possible to facilitate the efforts of your personnel from the time you first assign a task to them to when they complete it. This includes giving individuals authority to carry out assignments and ensuring that they feel free to approach you with questions.

b) **Delegate with deadlines.** When passing out assignments, remember Parkinson's Law: "Work expands to fill the time available for its completion." In other words, people tend to stretch out jobs as long as they can. To avoid procrastination and delay, directives to your staff should **never** be open-ended. Reasonable completion dates should always be specified.

I once worked with an executive who never established deadlines when making assignments. He had timelines in mind but did not share them with the rest of us. By not expressing his expectations, we never knew what was important to him and what was not important. The result: few assignments were completed in a timely fashion.

Besides helping the leader, delegating with deadlines benefits those given assignments. It frees the leader from constantly nagging staff members to complete assignments. They then can concentrate on tasks without interference or undue pressure.

Be sure to keep deadlines realistic. If your personnel keep missing deadlines for reasons beyond their control, they will soon start ignoring them.

c) **Create involvement in the assignment by asking for the individual's ideas and recommendations.** People perform better when their input is valued. The worst thing a leader can do is to delegate with a lot of advice on how to do the job. This kills initiative and creativity. For example, if you ask a staff member to prepare an analysis of the competitors in your industry and then proceed to tell him exactly what you want in the report, that is what you will get. Any additional information or intelligence that might have been obtained will be missing.

12. **Make every minute count for your personnel.** So far this chapter has focused on how you, the leader, can make the best use of your time. What about the time of your staff members? Their time is valuable too. Show consideration for them by being prompt to attend meetings. Avoid making them wait.

The best way to minimize such unproductive time is to provide some slack between your meetings and appointments just in case they run over. Your concern for the time of others will be appreciated and make them realize their importance too.

13. **Shield yourself from energy losses due to worrying.** Focusing on what someone else thinks of you, reorganization rumors, or some imagined slight from a colleague drains valuable energy needed to lead others. The key to combating worry is to become aware of your emotions. Only then can you keep things in proper perspective.

14. **Use planning devices.** Whether electronic or paper and pencil, the effective use of a planning device is crucial to managing your time well. Coordinate schedules with key team members as a regular part of your daily activities.

15. **Learn to utilize small chunks of time** that are normally wasted, such as waiting to board an airplane, standing in line at a supermarket, and waiting to pick up your kids. During such "dead times" read something of value or discuss important matters with another person. The most successful leaders never waste a moment.

16. **Get off to an early start each morning.** Possibly the most important timesaving advice is to begin work early each day. Arriving at work thirty minutes early provides valuable quiet time, uninterrupted by phone calls and associates wanting to talk. People who have the habit of starting work early claim by doing so, their entire day goes more smoothly.

Do not waste your high-energy hours. Invest them where they yield the highest payoff.

In review, you can improve your productivity and the productivity of your people by following the principles of time management presented in this chapter. Improvement can be accomplished without putting in more hours yourself. You might even surprise yourself by reducing some of the evening and weekend work that you previously thought was unavoidable. Most importantly, you will have more time to concentrate on the matters that really count: thinking strategically and interfacing with your people. With this in mind let us now turn our attention to the critically important topics of becoming more effective in dealing with others. In the next three chapters you will learn:

- How to earn the loyalty of team members,
- How to become more employee-centered, and
- How to do a better job of listening.

13

The Effective Leader Earns the Loyalty of Employees

The loyalty of your personnel is priceless. It cannot be bought or secured by favors. It is not won overnight nor is it everlasting. Rather, loyalty is given by the group as long as they think their leader is worthy of it.

Here are some ways to gain and hold the loyalty of your people:

Effective leaders make their followers feel good about themselves and their work.

1. **Develop person-to-person relationships with your team members.** Be approachable. This does not require that you become close personal friends. I have always felt that strong relationships can be built and maintained at work and at work alone. It is not necessary to frequently socialize after hours with your people to lead them successfully.

   However, you should take a few minutes each day to talk to team members on a personal level. Take an interest in the joys of their lives, whether it is their family, their hobbies, or their dreams for the future. Be open yourself by letting them learn a bit about the "you" that they don't see at work. Also, **smile more**. It will make you more approachable.

   Socializing with team members outside the office, however, can be counter-productive. Some team members may feel that this person is the boss's favorite. Other individuals who do not enjoy the same treatment could become jealous. There is also the possibility that a favored individual will take advantage of his or her special relationship with the boss.

Familiarity **can** breed contempt and erode respect for the leader. A certain psychological barrier must be maintained between the leader and the follower to ensure objectivity.

Whether or not you adopt this philosophy toward socializing privately with individual staff members, it is vitally important that you take a sincere and genuine interest in each person while you are with them at work.

The goal of the leader should be to develop mutual respect with team members.

A study reported in *Advances in Experimental Social Psychology* revealed that **showing genuine interest in people is the most important thing a leader can do to build and maintain the loyalty of his or her followers**. The best way to show interest in people is to give them your time. Freely sharing this most precious commodity demonstrates that you really care. If you care about your people, they will care about you.

2. **Be aggressive in serving your personnel.** All leaders should remember that their **primary** mission is to help their personnel be successful in **their** jobs. Providing such service involves clearing away obstacles that hinder performance, such as insufficient manpower or equipment, and showing people how to do their jobs more effectively.

Leaders are in the obstacle removal business.

In addition to helping your people succeed, look for other ways to serve them. This point is best illustrated by an experience I had several years ago in Edmonton. On a bitter cold January evening I arrived at the Purolator depot. In the short distance from the parking lot to the office I

The motto of a servant leader: "I am always here for you."

was chilled to the bone. It was difficult to breathe without the cold air causing discomfort to my lungs. Upon opening the door to the customer counter area, I found the depot manager putting on a heavy parka. "Where are you going on such a horrible night?" I asked. "Please excuse me for awhile," she replied. "Some of the couriers' cars won't start, and I need to help them." I thought to myself, "What commitment to others!"

Finally, pay attention to the physical comfort needs of your personnel. A hot office, dirty restrooms, or inadequate lighting might not be a big deal to you, but they are to others. It was a wise person indeed who once said, "It's not the mountain ahead that bothers the climber, but the grain of sand in the shoe."

Effective leaders follow the basic dictum of a West Pointer: Make sure the troops are settled and fed before you take care of your own needs.

The leader who is sensitive to the needs of his personnel is aggressive in quickly resolving minor complaints or concerns before they become major ones. If necessary, he will stick his neck out with superiors to obtain adequate resources and assistance for his people. The old adage that "the squeaky wheel gets the grease" applies to this facet of leadership. Employees do not have to work in plush surroundings to be content, but they do require leaders who look after their needs.

3. **Confide in the people you trust.** It is hard to be loyal to someone who is overly secretive. An individual feels important and special whenever the leader shares information about company business that is not generally known to others.

4. **Provide special rewards for your outstanding performers,** such as merit increases, strong recommendations for promotion, and recognition from you and your boss. High achievers need such treatment or they will lose interest and look elsewhere for employment.

Be proud of the accomplishments of your people. Always give them credit for their successes.

An excellent way to show appreciation for good work is to write letters of commendation for those teams and individuals who deserve credit. The advantage of letters is that the recipient can show them to co-workers, friends, and family. Be sure to send a copy to your manager and any other officials who might be interested. I call this "broadcast recognition." It places your people where they belong—in the spotlight.

Unselfishly giving well-deserved credit to your people is one of the finest things you can do for them. It not only makes them feel good, but stimulates them to try even harder.

5. **Recognize and show appreciation for other employees too.** Most leaders find it natural to recognize their high achievers. Yet, pressed with busy and demanding work schedules, you may easily overlook the many solid performers who quietly get the job done day-in, day-out. Because they do not require much supervision, the tendency is to take them for granted. These people also need to be recognized with periodic indications that their performance is acceptable and appreciated. A simple sincere demonstration of your interest in their work can go a long way toward keeping up their morale.

The best way to maintain morale is to meet individually with each of your team members at least once a week. If they are geographically dispersed, utilize the phone and "e-meetings" extensively. During this special one-on-one time give the person ample opportunity and encouragement to express anything on his or her mind. Look for things that are done right and acknowledge your understanding and appreciation for them. Further, **do not underestimate the power of a sincere thank you.**

The deepest principle in human nature is the craving to be appreciated.

William James

109

Several experiences in my career illustrate the power of appreciation and recognition. The first experience occurred in New York when I interviewed a courier who had received a letter of warning for excessive tardiness. I was intrigued by the fact that the person's attendance record had been excellent for a number of years prior to the recent problem. I asked him if he had personal problems at home that might have affected his ability to get to work on time. "No," he replied, "that's not the case." "What happened then to cause this sudden change in your behavior?" I asked. It took a moment or two for the courier to spill out his feelings about not being appreciated at work. Apparently parts of the job did not come easy to him, but he always tried to do his best. Never once did his manager offer a word of appreciation. *It's like I never existed in his eyes. So I did the only thing I could think of to get attention; I started coming in late. At first management didn't react to the change in my behavior. Now look what's happening. My boss has held several private discussions with me, and I get to talk with a senior vice-president.*

Shortly after the New York incident I was asked to speak at a district operations meeting. Prior to introducing me, the manager announced that she wanted to make several special recognition awards. She then proceeded to describe what each person had done and called him or her individually to the podium to receive a gift certificate. I will never forget the joyous expressions on the faces of those who received awards.

Stan, a manager for a major oil company, told me that he was so in need of recognition and appreciation from his boss that he once wrote on a copy of one of **his** oil exploration studies:

"Excellent work, Stan." He then sent it to a number of his peers in his division. Stan was so starved for recognition that he had to praise **himself!**

Although praise and recognition are powerful motivators, they should never be used in lieu of pay increases. Motivating employees requires both praise and tangible rewards. The effective leader does not stint on either.

The praise and reward, however, must be carefully selected. The successful leader determines which rewards or incentives are most meaningful to each person. What motivates one person does not necessarily motivate another. For example, an ambitious person may crave opportunities to learn new skills as quickly as possible to become more promotable. Another staff member who is struggling to balance career and family needs might value flexible hours or the opportunity to work at home a day or two a week. Still another might simply need to be periodically reassured that his work is valued and appreciated. The point is that the leader needs to tailor the reward system to each individual.

6. **Show respect for team members** by valuing their opinions even though they may be different from your own. Your personnel must feel safe to disagree with you, even in front of others.

What we have done for ourselves alone dies with us. What we have done for others and the world remains and is immortal.

Albert Pine

In summary, the best way to gain and hold the loyalty of your personnel is to serve them by showing interest in them, caring for them, and helping them succeed. And this attitude of concern must be sincere. **Your people will never be totally loyal unless they know deep down that you are devoted to the good of all and are doing everything in your power to serve them.**

14

The Effective Leader Is Employee Centered

The great paradox of life: The more you give of yourself, the more you receive.

Employee-centered leaders are sensitive to the needs and feelings of their people. They are supportive of employees, helpful to them, and concerned for their well being. Such leaders subordinate their own interests to those of others.

The principle focus in business remains on making a profit. Obviously, you cannot keep people gainfully employed unless the company prospers. The problem arises when decisions revolve solely on the basis of profit without due consideration to the people-issues involved. Worse yet are the decisions made at the expense of employees. Invariably, such shortsighted approaches do not stimulate the kind of teamwork and extra effort required to be competitive in today's global market. When employees feel abused or when they do not feel valued, they tend to do just enough to get by.

For a people-first philosophy to capture the heart and soul of an organization, it must be based on the fundamental belief and practice that people are cared for and treated with dignity first and foremost because it is the right thing to do.

David Sarnoff, former chairman of RCA, identified the most important by-product of being employee centered. He said: "We accomplish greatness through other people." And managers who try to lead by virtue of position cannot achieve this greatness.

Many employees today do not have the same strong loyalty to their employers that their parents had. Workers are now likely to come and go based on pay rates, opportunities to learn, and, most importantly, the satisfaction they receive from the job. This satisfaction is derived from having interesting tasks, being involved and learning new skills—all of which lead to a feeling of worth.

Morale and productivity are therefore highest in work groups when the leader provides the opportunities mentioned above plus when he shows a high degree of **consideration** and **concern** for everyone. This requires that the leader understand that each team member is the center of his or her own universe; each person has unique needs, interests, likes, and dislikes.

Be a leader with heart!

Most people appreciate a leader who takes a sincere interest in them, who responds in some appropriate manner to the great joys and sorrows that occur in their lives. The idea is not to be nosey and constantly prying into employees' personal lives, but to be responsive in a warm human way when you get word of a serious personal problem.

Share your inner gifts with your people—your warmth, sensitivity, and enthusiasm.

Frank Borman, the former astronaut who headed Eastern Airlines in the 1980's, went out of his way to demonstrate that he cared for his employees. For several years I worked for him as his executive assistant. One evening when I returned from a business trip, I found his car parked in my driveway. Obviously, I was very concerned that something serious had happened, as he had never visited my home. When I entered the back door, I found him playing in the family room with my three-year-old daughter, Cindy, who was recovering from knee surgery. He had brought a teddy bear to cheer her up. Even today it remains one of the most cherished gifts that she ever received.*

Joita McGlynn, a former Eastern employee, relates another touching story about Borman. Her sister, Missy, who was seriously ill, asked Joita if she could meet her "big boss." Joita took her to Miami to do so. When Borman learned of the situation, he gladly offered to see them. After talking to Joita and Missy for a while, Borman said, "I'd now like to spend some time with Missy alone, so it will be her special time."

Contrast these demonstrations of caring concern with an incident that occurred in another company several years later. While working on a construction site, a man was struck by a falling tile that caused cuts and lacerations. He was immediately rushed to the hospital and later released to spend several days at home to recuperate. A number of his co-workers sent cards and called him. Yet, the one person who counted most, his manager, never inquired about his welfare. Just as Cindy and Missy will never forget Frank Borman's thoughtfulness, the man struck by the tile will never forget his manager's insensitivity and lack of concern.

If you remember only one thought from this chapter, it should be: **Handle an employee's problem swiftly and as seriously as if it were a problem with your own paycheck.** Most of you, I am sure, have experienced a situation where your paycheck was late, lost, or shorted. Remember how quickly you called the payroll department or asked your manager to fix the problem. Treat the problems of your personnel with the same concern and urgency.

Being employee centered also means being **fair**— treating others as you would like to be treated. The results of numerous surveys in major corporations

Build a reservoir of goodwill by placing the interests of your people above your own.

point out that getting a fair deal is the most important concern to employees at all levels. Even the slightest hint of favoritism can poison the morale of an organization. Showing more warmth to team members you like or spending more time with them can be demoralizing to others who perceive that they are not in your favor. The cardinal rule is: **play no favorites.**

In review, the effective leader has the ability to make others feel good about themselves by the degree of consideration, concern, and equity shown. Attending to these feelings creates a strong bond between the leader and his or her followers.

* Years have now passed since Frank Borman dropped off the teddy bear to Cindy. During this time many people have read the story in this book and I've used the story in numerous speeches and training programs as an example of the power of caring leadership. When Borman retired, I wrote him a note to let him know how much his kind act of caring for Cindy had favorably influenced the lives of so many people.

15

The Effective Leader Listens Actively

Make people feel important by listening carefully to them.

Listening attentively and empathetically is one of the best ways to show respect for a member of your team. It demonstrates that you believe the individual has worthwhile thoughts and therefore is valued. When people feel needed, they tend to take more interest in what they do.

Empathetic listening does more than facilitate employee motivation. It helps protect the leader from being blindsided. Employees will not open up to leaders who are aloof or too busy to spend time listening. Without the knowledge of what staff members really think and believe, the leader is vulnerable to the sudden surfacing of a major morale problem. By listening carefully to employees' perceptions of problems, you can resolve them before they escalate.

An office manager of an accounting firm was uncomfortable relating to first-level personnel. Instead of listening to them directly, he relied on his supervisors' interpretations of their concerns. Frustrated, the employees wrote their complaints to the president of the company. The problems that could have been resolved easily at a lower level of management were now the topic of discussion with upper management.

By insulating himself from first-level personnel, the manager did not know what was going on in his operation. Had he kept the channels of communication open at all levels and listened through the grapevine deep within the organization, he could have identified the problems early and taken corrective action.

According to James MacGregor Burns: "Few executive leaders have better exemplified the strengths and weaknesses of personnel management than Franklin Roosevelt. Some said he had a discerning, intuitive grasp of the needs and motivations of his cabinet members and agency chiefs. One of his many traits—difficult for a man who loved to talk and dominate the scene—was to listen sympathetically to those who poured out their woes and frustrations."[1]

Whenever General Eisenhower was faced with a difficult problem, he would call his staff together and take great pains to listen to their ideas and recommendations. It is reported that President Kennedy failed to solicit adequate discussion about the Bay of Pigs issue before deciding to go ahead with the operation. He changed his approach, however, during the Cuban missile crisis when he actively sought divergent opinions before taking action.

These stories illustrate a vital principle about listening and communicating in general: Leaders who make it a practice to draw out the thoughts and ideas of their personnel and who are receptive even to bad news will be properly informed. Having the "straight-scoop" and all the appropriate information is very important to the leader's ability to make good decisions.

All of us prefer good news to bad. Few people will voluntarily present all the details of bad news if their bosses become upset and sore. Instead, there will be a tendency to cover up or sugarcoat the facts. Leaders who follow the advice of welcoming the messenger of bad news (instead of shooting him) will be well ahead of the game in the communications area.

A number of approaches and techniques will improve your listening skills. Here are some that I find useful:

1. Try to interpret more than the surface conversation of the speaker to determine his true feelings and

thoughts. In the presence of their manager, many people will not open up and express what is on their minds. Instead they will couch their words to refrain from stepping on someone else's toes. Since frank communication is vital to the success of any organization, the leader must be able to draw out the feelings of team members by listening sympathetically.

2. Be an active listener:

a) Assume an attentive attitude—stand up or sit up straight, directly face the speaker, and maintain good eye contact.

b) Take notes, if appropriate to do so.

c) Ask pertinent questions and rephrase key points that are made (e.g., "Do you mean that . . . ," or "My understanding of what you just said is . . ."). Do this in a manner that does not give the impression that you have already made up your mind about what was said or are looking for an argument.

3. Wait until you clearly understand what a person is saying before you reply.

4. Show respect for the individual who is talking by refraining from discourteous, nonverbal behavior such as glancing at your watch, letting your eyes wander, shuffling papers, or starting for the door. These actions signal a lack of interest to someone who is trying to relate something important.

5. Control your desire to do the talking. There is no way you can listen while speaking.

6. Draw out the individual by asking his opinions or ideas on a subject. If discussion on a performance problem is required, refrain from criticizing the qualities of the person, such as his integrity or intelligence. Focus instead on what can be done to prevent the problem from happening again. Very little meaningful conversation occurs when people feel attacked or threatened.

The most important good listening habit is to totally concentrate on what the person is saying.

7. Listen to everyone, not just to those whom you like. It is easy to fall into the trap of giving attention to high producers and ignoring average performers. This practice can hurt morale and cause some people to remain quiet even though they have something important to contribute.

8. Do not jump to conclusions after the first few sentences are spoken. This conveys that you are really not interested in what they have to say. Instead, hear them out. Only then will you fully understand what is on their minds.

9. Avoid the temptation to interrupt the other person to make your own comments or points. You may not agree with what the individual is saying, but you must allow him to say it. It is remarkable how many problems and concerns dissolve when people are given the opportunity to get things off their chests.

10. Minimize telephone interruptions by conducting important conversations away from your desk. I often do this by holding meetings in conference rooms where I can give the other person my undivided attention. If this is impractical, silence your phone and let voice mail catch your calls. There is nothing more distracting than a ringing phone when you are trying to discuss a serious matter.

Remember that listening attentively and empathically is one of the best ways to build trust with individuals in your organization. As previously mentioned in other parts of the book, **trust means everything in leadership.**

16

The Effective Leader Is Determined

PRESS ON. Nothing in the world can take the place of persistence. Talent will not; nothing is more common than unsuccessful men with talent. Genius will not; unrewarded genius is a proverb. Education will not; the world is full of educated derelicts. Persistence and determination alone are omnipotent.

Calvin Coolidge

High-performing leaders exhibit exceptional determination in pursuing their objectives. They never let up until they succeed. A study of Nobel Prize winners in science revealed that what distinguishes the winners from their colleagues is remarkable determination.

There is no better example than Thomas Edison, who in April 1872 worked continuously day and night to find a way to permit simultaneous two-way transmission on a telephone line. Suffering from exhaustion, he was about ready to give up. On the twenty-second day, he found the solution.

Hugh Sidney, writing in *Time* magazine, describes George Washington's role at the Battle of Trenton as follows:

Three columns were to have crossed the Delaware River; only Washington's made it across. The powder of his troops was soaked by a freezing rain, so they could not fire their arms. They had to defend with bayonets several times during the night. Washington's officers pleaded with him to call off the attack. The story goes that he stood on an old beehive in a muddy New Jersey field and turned aside every petition to retreat. The Battle of Trenton was won by the determination of this leader![1]

Brigadier General Billy Mitchell also exemplified this important quality of leadership. At age thirty-nine Mitchell commanded a fighter squadron on the Eastern front in World War I. He strongly pushed for innovative ideas, such as forming large bomber armadas to destroy enemy formations, and parachuting men and guns behind enemy lines. His ideas were so radical that it took great drive and persistence to convince superiors to try them.[2]

After the war Mitchell dedicated his life to the cause of promoting the concept of a separate air force to defend the country. His use of the press to gain support so incensed the top Army brass that he was court-martialed for insubordination in 1925.[3] Thirty years later "Congress voted Mitchell a posthumous medal for his foresight in the field of aviation."[4]

Nellie Bly, the well-known reporter for the *New York World* in the early 1900's, had a similar sense of urgency. Despite the warnings of friends and enemies, she could not be kept from investigating the graft and corruption that was found in high places in city government.

Another charismatic leader, Teddy Roosevelt, had one trait that overshadowed everything else: determination. As a child, he was small, had poor eyesight, and suffered from severe asthma. In his autobiography Roosevelt noted that he often lay in his bed struggling to breathe, afraid that he would not awaken in the morning. Weakened by his illness, he had to rely on Elliott, his younger brother, to shield him from the neighborhood bullies.[5]

Nevertheless, Teddy willed himself to become strong, both mentally and physically. Each day he pushed himself; he spent hours lifting weights and doing chin-ups. Interested in a wide variety of subjects, he read every book he could get his hands on. By the time he enrolled in Harvard, Roosevelt had become a man of extreme energy and enthusiasm. Faculty and students alike described him as being forceful and colorful.[6]

Numerous other people achieved unusual success in their lives by sheer force of their determination. R. H. Macy had seven retail failures before his store in New York became successful. In 1922, Harry Truman was thirty-eight, in debt, and unemployed. Twenty-three years later he was the President of the United States. Basketball superstar Michael Jordan never gave up on his ambition to play in the NBA—even after being cut from his high school team. Few people realize how difficult a time Walt Disney had in launching his exceptional career. He was fired from a newspaper position for "lack of creativity" and later became bankrupt several times.[7] Finally, according to James C. Humes, author of a biography on Winston Churchill: "Few people realize that Churchill never could get into any university and had such a congenital lisp and stutter that doctors advised him against entering an occupation in which speaking was an important part." Yet history remembers him as a voice that breathed hope into a frightened, discouraged country under siege.

At this point I can almost hear you saying: "It's great that famous people like Mitchell, Roosevelt, Truman, Jordan, Disney, and Churchill persevered to overcome tremendous obstacles in their lives; but what about me? I've got problems that can't be solved." This may be true at present, but more often than not, most difficulties in life can be resolved over time if the **will** is there to do it. In this area one can take great comfort from a passage from Dr. Norman Vincent Peale's famous book, *The Power of Positive Thinking.* The following words have helped me time and time again in my life:

This is a fact that you must never forget. . . . there are people who have overcome every conceivable difficult situation even like the one in which you now find yourself and which to you seems utterly hopeless. . . . but somehow they found an out, a way up, a path over, a pass through.

In the business world you often need more than just sheer determination to succeed. You need to couple determination with a sense of timing. Knowing when to push for changes and improvements often determines the success of obtaining them. Most of us have heard the phrase: "An idea whose time has come." People are not always psychologically ready to accept innovative ideas. Knowing when the time is right takes a degree of astuteness and patience.

Shortly after joining Federal Express, my staff and I developed recommendations for various types of sales incentive programs for our couriers. The objective was to inspire the couriers to increase their efforts to obtain new customers. For various reasons the proposals were turned down.

One morning about a year later Pete Willmott, the president of the company, came by my office. At the time, we were experiencing a shortfall in revenue from the business plan. After saying hello he immediately said, "You've just got to find a way to increase revenue." "Give us a few days, and we'll have a solution," I replied. Realizing that Pete was finally ready to consider any reasonable approach, the best ideas from several earlier proposals were revised into a comprehensive, new plan. A few days later it was approved.

The lesson: **With determination and timing you cannot lose!**

Genius is eternal patience.
　　Michelangelo

To know how to wait is one of the great secrets of success.
　　James DeMaistre

To everything there is a season.
　　Ecclesiastes 3:1

17

The Effective Leader Is Available and Visible to His or Her Team

The front line is the only place where you can truly understand the nature of what's happening in a business.

One of the most important maxims of leadership is: **Be there with your personnel.** Sometimes that is difficult—especially when employees work on shifts. Keeping sixteen hour schedules talking to employees on shifts is taxing, but I have found it an important way to raise employee morale and to understand operations.

The great lesson of leadership from the military is that the troops will put up with a difficult life, often with intolerable conditions, if their leaders visibly do the same. History is full of examples of the impact of the commander's presence on the front lines:

- General Robert E. Lee made it a practice to visit the campsites of his troops the night before each major battle. Often he would do this at the expense of getting sleep himself.
- General Patton was often seen riding the lead tank of his armor units. His daring courage was an inspiration to his men.
- The Duke of Wellington, who defeated Napoleon at Waterloo, believed that Napoleon's presence on the battlefield was worth 40,000 soldiers.[1]

What applies in the military also applies to running a business. According to Thomas Peters and Robert H. Waterman, Jr., co-authors of *In Search of Excel-*

lence, "management by wandering around" may be the most important thing managers can do to improve work quality and productivity. This involves frequently chatting with employees on-the-job to learn first-hand what is necessary to improve performance. A feel for the subtleties of the business cannot be obtained by reading reports or financial statements. Rather, it requires direct and frequent input from personnel at all levels.

Just wandering around is of little value unless you utilize the time to inspire and guide employees. This is accomplished by taking a sincere interest in each person. **Your attitude is the key**. It is demonstrated every day by the dignity shown each person, the concern expressed for someone's personal problem, and the appreciation given to those who give extra effort.

One of the major benefits of spending time with your people is that it enables you to detect and act upon negative employee attitudes before they spread and create morale problems. It is difficult for someone to continually disguise ill feelings toward the job or the organization. In one way or another the negative attitudes will be expressed with words or actions. Just the simple matter of how neat the workplace is kept or how the equipment is treated tells a great deal about the status of group morale.

Your role as leader is to determine the causes of negative employee attitudes and take early corrective action. Sometimes it is as simple as clearing up a misunderstanding or providing additional training. In other cases it may be necessary to do a better job of fulfilling an individual's need for recognition or providing opportunities for them to perform more challenging assignments. Occasionally, it may be necessary to confront an individual directly and let him know that you will not tolerate his attitude. In short,

A desk is a dangerous place from which to watch the world.

John le Carre

you must quickly isolate the source of negativism and eliminate it. Otherwise, your department will never be a winner.

The extent to which you should involve yourself in your operation depends on your level in the organization. If you are a first-level manager, you should spend at least 70 percent of your time with your people. Senior officers should devote at least a full day a week to making field visitations. The key to effective visits is to institute them on a regular schedule. On such visits make sure you meet with all levels of employees. Dedicate quality time for listening and sharing ideas concerning service and operations.

When walking around an operation, you must be careful not to embarrass the manager in front of his personnel by making comments about performance problems. The best approach is to keep your observations to yourself until you can arrange a private discussion with the manager.

Your primary mission during a plant or office visitation should be to get a feel for employee esprit de corps—the level of morale, pride and enthusiasm. This cannot be accomplished by a brief guided tour with you saying hello to employees as you walk past their work areas. Nor is it possible when accompanied by members of local management. Employees just will not be candid in front of their immediate bosses. A comprehensive visit takes several hours, which should be divided between formal meetings and chatting privately with individuals.

Your secondary mission during a visitation should be to reinforce the company's core values concerning the treatment of employees and customers. **Values are needed in organizations to guide people in their daily actions**. The leader should take every opportunity to reinforce the values of honesty, mutual

I always return from field visits with the feeling that I have learned something important.

respect for others, and pride in the quality of production and service.

Grace Pastiak, Director of Manufacturing for Tellabs Inc., credits her success with her habit of continually communicating the value of excellent workmanship to her employees. She frequently visits the plant employees with the goal of "trying to infect them with a zeal for producing high quality products."[2]

Herb Kelleher, Chairman of Southwest Airlines, demonstrates his company's value that employees are important by giving up his discretionary time to meet with them around the clock. Herb prefers to conduct informal sessions in the work setting rather than to hold formal meetings. Tom Burnett, a union official, compliments Herb on his style of direct, open communications: "How many CEO's do you know who come into cleaners' breakroom at 3 a.m. on a Sunday to talk?"[3]

Like radar, the good leader picks up obvious and not so obvious signals about conditions in an operation.

When conducting employee meetings, listen carefully to the type of questions asked. If most questions concern local conditions, such as work assignments or vacation schedules, it usually indicates that first-level management is not adequately taking care of employee needs. If the questions focus on broader matters, such as corporate plans or strategies, it could mean one of two things: either the employees' concerns are being adequately addressed or they are so intimidated by local management that they are afraid to bring up specific work problems. If you sense that it is intimidation, you need to probe further in private conversations with individuals.

Sometimes you will encounter a shy group that will not ask questions or express their concerns. If so, try asking open-ended questions:

- What is preventing your team or section from being the best?

- What can we do to better support your efforts?

What might you need to know more about?

If you project a warm, friendly image when asking these questions, you will receive all the feedback you need.

Besides conducting employee meetings during plant or office visitations, make it a practice to randomly select several people to talk with privately. Even a few one-on-one discussions can provide a good indication of the group's moral.

You know things are going well when the group's accomplishments are frequently mentioned. Look for what is said or not said about the group's manager. If nothing is said, dig deeper. Favorable, unsolicited comments given in private are a positive sign of high morale.

Things are often not what they first appear to be.

When holding such conversations, be careful to separate the "wheat from the chaff"—important concerns or complaints from those that are not. Periodically, you will meet an employee with a bad attitude or one that can never be pleased. This is to be expected. What you should be interested in is feedback from a number of people that, in total, can paint an overall picture of a group's esprit de corps.

When an employee expresses a grievance, take it seriously. Listen intently and ask questions for clarification. Then indicate your willingness to investigate further. Finally, give the employee an idea when you will get back with him or her. **Never fail to keep this promise.**

In summary, successful leaders always find time to make the rounds, chat with their personnel, show an interest in them, and listen to their concerns and ideas. This is not just a nice thing to do; it is a necessity to achieve excellence in an organization.

V

The Three Key Requirements for Peak Leadership Performance

So far, I have discussed seventeen characteristics of effective leaders. Emulating these traits is a worthwhile strategy for anyone who wants to lead others successfully. Unfortunately, leadership entails more than acquiring isolated characteristics. Other conditions contribute to and sustain leadership excellence over the long run.

Just as a flowering plant will fail to bloom year after year unless there are proper levels of sunlight, moisture, and nutrients, so a person will not reach his full leadership potential unless he

- is healthy,
- has a satisfactory personal life, and
- is committed to life-long learning.

Certainly, one or more of these conditions can be absent from the leader's life for several months or even longer. All human beings have occasional health and personal problems; their motivation to learn also lapses. However, no one can consistently perform at his best if plagued by persistent ill-health or emotionally draining problems at home. This leads to a preoccupation with self, which interferes with one's ability to be empathic and involved with others.

A person can have the best health and personal life imaginable and still not achieve leadership success unless he is committed to life-long self-development. When personal growth and development ceases, leaders can become as obsolete as a five-year-old PC.

For organizations to thrive and flourish, management must always seek the best leadership available. Weaknesses or failures in leadership cannot be tolerated for long. In time, effective new leaders must be found.

In the following three chapters you will learn about specific actions you can take to reach your full leadership potential. You will learn how to keep your health, build a fulfilling personal life, and be a life-long learner.

VI

How to Keep Your Health by Managing Stress

From a survey of nine thousand workers from companies and public service organizations, a startling discovery was made. More than 45 percent of the respondents said they suffered from burnout—a disabling reaction to job stress. According to Robert Golembiewski, who led the survey team, "These people were in pretty bad shape and felt high levels of emotional exhaustion."[1]

Leaders, particularly those on the way up in their organizations, are susceptible to high levels of stress. Not only do they have their own problems to worry about, but also those of their team members. Acting as a shepherd to others is emotionally draining. Different personalities have to be handled with sensitivity. Various personnel needs have to be addressed daily. Leaders are also faced with continuous pressure to produce favorable results. Finally, tension arises in constantly striving to get that next promotion.

Few tasks are more important to the leader than the effective management of stress. It is necessary for the leader to function effectively and to assist team members to do the same. Helping employees handle stress can yield substantial improvements in their job satisfaction and productivity.

This chapter provides insights into the nature of stress, how to spot it, and how to manage it.

WHAT CAUSES STRESS?

When the mind perceives a situation as disagreeable, dangerous, or bad, it triggers the body's glands to release large quantities of the hormones cortisone and adrenaline. When these hormones are released, physiological changes occur, such as sharpened reflexes, heavy breathing, increased blood pressure, and a more rigid heart rate. In effect, the body becomes mobilized for action and the threatened individual is able to react with increased strength and speed. This is called the "fight or flight syndrome." [2]

We experience many stress reactions each day. We rush to meet deadlines, we try to solve unexpected problems, and we experience bad news.

Being human, many people worry about their jobs during the day and dream about them at night. They wake up tight and tense, with less capacity to deal with new problems. This is the beginning of a vicious cycle leading to burnout.

From an analysis of the lifestyles of 1,200 centenarians, it was concluded that the avoidance of stress was a common denominator of longevity.

When stressful conditions cause you to stay "hyped up" for prolonged periods and when the stress is not relieved, the body begins to deteriorate. Since the body functions as an integrated system, a breakdown will occur at the weakest link, causing pain or illness. At this point your body is sending you a vital message: "Slow down, reduce your stress or else." If you heed the message and take appropriate action, your body, like a coil spring, will return to a normal condition. However, failure to act could eventually result in serious illness.

OTHER IMPORTANT FACTS ABOUT STRESS

The trick is to function with a level of stress that is life enhancing—not life threatening.

1. A certain amount of stress is important for life to have meaning. As an activation response, stress is a form of energy that is required for people to function effectively. Stress is necessary for us to have productive, happy lives. It keeps us on our toes; helps us forget minor physical irritations, and provides a sense of exhilaration when we accomplish things in tight time frames. Without some stress, we become easily bored and lack direction. Often this is the problem of a newly retired executive. Suddenly, he or she does not have to make the effort each day to go to work and handle challenging assignments. Monotony from a pur-

poseless existence can be as discomforting as a high level of stress.

2. What causes stress is a highly individual matter. For example, giving a performance appraisal is stressful to many managers who dislike evaluating people. Other managers view appraisals as an opportunity to guide and help their team members. Losing an important promotion could cause one person to become despondent and another to redouble his efforts.

An individual's capacity for stress also varies. It depends on a number of factors including physical and emotional health, personality characteristics, and past experience in handling stressful situations.

3. It is not the single stressful event that harms people, but long-term stress built up at increasingly higher, uninterrupted levels. Continuous stress gradually destroys a person's capacity to solve problems and often leads to illness.

Without stress resistance, the manager will change course to avoid problems, surrender to defeat, or dash himself to pieces.[4]

According to the American Medical Association, "80 percent of our diseases are either caused by or aggravated by stress."[3] These diseases range from minor ailments (e.g., aches and pains) to life-threatening diseases (e.g., strokes, heart attacks, and cancer). Stress can even weaken one's immune system.

STRESS WARNING SIGNS

Some people become so accustomed to running their engines at full speed that they do not realize that their bodies are reacting adversely. They may ignore important warning signs manifested by a change in behavior, appearance, or physical sensation.

In his book *The Stress of Life,* Hans Selye identifies thirty-one stress-warning signs. Some of the most common are:

- Impatience and irritability
- Exhaustion—even when getting adequate sleep
- Acting dogmatic and abusive
- Insomnia
- Frequent constipation
- Unusual numbers of colds, flu, etc.
- Restlessness—even at home
- Rapid heart beat
- Indigestion, stomach pains, backaches
- Loss of appetite
- Difficulty in concentrating—disjointed thinking
- Neglect of physical appearance
- Loss of optimism
- Tendency to avoid or withdraw from difficult situations or problems
- Feeling run-down or tired for long periods

ENVIRONMENTAL CONDITIONS THAT COULD LEAD TO STRESS

In general, stress results from feelings of being pressured, of losing control over events, and of being uncertain about the future. These feelings can occur in your private life or at work. Some of the more stressful situations include:

- Death or serious illness in the family
- Divorce or separation
- Unrealistic expectations about career success
- Problems with children
- Family conflict
- Personal injury or illness
- Constant pressure, both self-imposed and boss-imposed
- Uncertainty over job security
- Doing work that you do not like or are unsuited for
- Pressure to compromise your principles for the sake of your career

- Excessive change
- Frequent travel over time zones
- Being blocked from promotional opportunities
- Poor relationship with immediate manager

WAYS TO PREVENT EXCESSIVE STRESS

A certain amount of stress is inevitable in our lives. There will always be some tension and conflict because of the imperfect nature of the universe we live in. Everything just does not run smoothly all the time. However, since an individual's reactions to stress are learned, they can be unlearned. In short, modifying habits and attitudes can minimize the effects of stress.

The first step in managing stress is to develop an awareness of being under excessive stress. Learn to recognize the warning signs previously presented. The short-term stress reactions associated with tense events (such as giving speeches, confronting problem employees, or making difficult decisions) are part of the job, but the continued feeling of pressure or tension that gradually builds up over time should, and can be, avoided.

It is helpful to recognize which situations or events in your life cause you the most stress. (See previous lists.) If you are more aware of what causes stress and can recognize when you are under excessive stress, you will be better able to control it.

There are a number of specific strategies for managing stress. In general, they are centered on (a) gaining control over your life, (b) maintaining good health habits, and (c) finding ways to release tension and enjoy yourself.

A. DEVELOP A SENSE OF CONTROL IN YOUR LIFE. The inability to have a high degree of autonomy in life leads to tension and stress. Autonomy means the freedom to pursue your own goals in life and to manage your affairs as you see fit. In the movie *Middle Age Crazy,* a father who has just turned forty begins to feel his life is controlled by others: his demanding sign installation business, a doting wife, and relatives with personal problems. Unable to cope with all the strings tying him down, he angrily tells his wife, "I'm tired of being the daddy to everyone."

Losing options is one of life's greatest stresses.[5]

Emotionally healthy people maintain a high degree of control over what happens in their lives. They take the initiative and make things happen. They do not wait for good luck; they create it.

Emotionally stable people seem to have one more trait in common. They maintain a big picture perspective about life. They view the whole as good and decent and do not overreact to the normal strains of daily living.

Some other suggestions for gaining better control of your life include:

1. **Confront your problems head on rather than avoiding them.** Often you are better off to act and get things behind you than to procrastinate and stew about them. As William James said, "Nothing is so fatiguing as the eternal hanging on of an uncompleted task."

2. **Live in the present and look forward to the future.** Be at peace with yourself. Do not waste valuable time or energy worrying about what you could have done differently in the past. Nothing can be done about the yesterdays of your life. Decide to be happy today, to make the best of what you have—your family, job, and friends. Words from a poem from the *Sanskrit* say it all:

Live today well, look to the morrow with vision and hope.
Bonnie Bailey

The Salutation of the Dawn

Listen to the exhortation of the dawn! Look to this day! For it is life, the very life of life. In its brief course lie all the verities and

> *realities of your existence: the bliss of growth, the glory of action, the splendor of beauty; For yesterday is but a dream, and tomorrow is only a vision. But today well lived makes every tomorrow a vision of hope. Look well, therefore, to this day! Such is the salutation of the dawn.*

Therefore, each morning when you awake try to start the day with a clean slate. Feel that you are free to act and do as you choose. You can choose to be cheerful, or you can choose to be sad. You can choose to be loving and caring, or you can choose to be hateful and selfish. It is up to you!

3. **Do not try to be all things to all people** by accepting every request to participate in volunteer work. A leader needs some time each day to unwind and enjoy family and friends. Attending too many civic and community functions at night just adds to stress. Instead, focus on a few volunteer projects that you enjoy. Dr. Herbert Freudenberger, a noted author and psychoanalyst, has a unique way of deciding to undertake or turn down an additional activity. Prior to making such a decision he asks himself: "If I had only one more year to live, would I do it?"[6]

Stop trying to please everyone.

4. **Think positive thoughts.** There is an increasing body of evidence that people with a positive outlook on life have more energy and better health than those preoccupied with negative thinking. According to Daniel Goleman, author of *Emotional Intelligence:* "People who have hopefulness, understandably, are better able to bear up under trying circumstances including medical difficulties."[7] He adds, "Studies show far more optimists survive heart attacks than pessimists."[8]

If you look for the positive things in life, you'll find them.

141

There are a number of ways you can train your-self to think more positive thoughts. First, whenever you encounter a setback or disappointment, look for what can be learned from the situation that will help yield improved results in the future. Then say to yourself something like: "What I learned today will someday be invaluable." Second, make it a practice to look for the good qualities in people and then let them know how you feel about them. For example, if you encounter a store salesperson or a restaurant waiter with a friendly, positive attitude, compliment him. If one of your work associates demonstrates a high level of determination or as-tuteness in handling a difficult situation, express your admiration.

The third way to concentrate on the positive as-pects of life is to practice what Dr. Robert Schuller calls "possibility thinking." He says, "In everything you encounter in life look for what could be or the possibilities for success." For example, if someone comes to you with an idea for a new approach or system, focus your initial thoughts and comments on the possibilities of it succeeding. There is al-ways time later on to consider why the idea might not work. If you consciously put "possibility thinking" first, it won't be long until it becomes a part of your general nature.

Finally, whenever you get discouraged or "a bit down," think of something positive in your life. Let your mind drift to an incident or occasion in the past that was particularly pleasant. For example, let good memories with your family be triggered by such stimuli as children playing baseball in a park, the aroma of a cake baking, or a choir singing. Such images release pent-up tension by creating a feeling of warmth and love.

5. **Re-examine your lifestyle** to determine if it is really worth the stress and tension that occurs from constantly striving to move up the management ladder. If you think money will eventually buy contentment, you are headed for a bitter disappointment. Money helps smooth the way, but it does not buy you friendships and the affection of your family. These are secured by taking the **time** to love and care.

Make money your God, and it will plague you like the devil.

Henry Fielding

Be realistic about your career possibilities. Everyone cannot be a division VP or head of their company. At some point in your life, you need to take stock of what you can realistically achieve. Come to terms with yourself by setting a limit on what you are willing to do for job success.

Therefore do not be anxious about tomorrow for tomorrow will be anxious for itself. Let the day's own trouble be sufficient for the day.

Matthew 6:34

Adopting a philosophy of doing the best you can and letting the chips fall as they may is necessary to avoid harmful stress. Isabel Moore expresses the same philosophy in a slightly different way: "Life is a one-way street. No matter how many detours you take, none of them leads back. And once you know and accept that, life becomes much simpler."

6. **Never use drugs or alcohol to help gain control in your life**. They make problems worse.

So far I've presented six suggestions for gaining better control of your life. Leaders should realize that their employees have a similar need to develop a sense of control in **their** lives. The best way to help people in this area is to keep them constantly informed about developments in the company that might affect them. Having factual information helps individuals feel in control of circumstances.

B. MAINTAIN GOOD HEALTH HABITS

Remember how you felt about your body when you were in high school or college? Chances are you were fifteen to twenty-five pounds lighter and in good shape. You felt good physically, and this influenced your entire attitude about life. According to Ralph LaForge, Managing Director of Preventive Medicine at Sharp Memorial Hospital: "By initiating only one healthy behavior—exercise—you'll begin to change a whole gamut of additional healthy behaviors without even trying. You'll tend to eat better, sleep better, and take better care of yourself. And as a result, you'll also experience an improvement in your self-image."[9] All of these benefits of exercise help moderate stress.

Peter Jensen, co-founder of the Center for High Performance in Ontario, goes even further in praising the benefits of exercise. He says: "People who are mentally fit—who have a mind-set fueled by being physically fit—can open doors to success that many of us only dream of."[10]

Dr. Ralph S. Paffenbarger, Jr., of the Stanford School of Medicine, says, "Exercise during middle age can actually retard physiological aging. Activity seems to lengthen life, maybe one or two years. We can expect that for every hour you're active, you will get to live that hour over—and possibly two more on top of that."[11]

One of the frequently heard excuses for not exercising is that "it just takes too long." Actually, medical tests indicate that it does not take much time to keep fit. Fifteen minutes a day of concentrated exercise has nearly the same training affect as an hour's workout.[12]

How does physical activity fight stress? Exercise burns off the hormones that produce stress.[13] Fifteen minutes of strenuous exercise can be tranquilizing and stimulate creativity.[14]

What is good for your health is good for your performance.

Peter Jensen

People who exercise regularly do not experience significant disturbances in their physical health and emotional well being during periods of high stress.[15]

Jonathon D. Brown, Ph.D.

Aerobic exercise (such as swimming, jogging, cycling, and brisk walking) is an ideal way to fight stress because it leads to sustained increases in heart rate and breathing without placing undue strain on the heart.

Considering the heavy time demands on leaders, the best approach is to work out five or six days a week for about fifteen to twenty minutes at a time. Exercise aerobically to get your pulse rate up continuously for this period. The key to maintaining a regular exercise program is to find an activity that is enjoyable and then stick with it.

Assuming you have the necessary self-discipline, it is relatively easy to establish an exercise routine at home. It is quite another matter to do so when traveling on business. Leaders who travel spend most of their time attending meetings during the day and entertaining at night. The combination of inactivity, inadequate sleep, and a propensity to eat rich foods has one result: poor health. With most evenings unavailable for exercise, one solution is to work out in the early morning by either jogging or using, if available, the hotel exercise room.

Men in poor physical condition are four times more likely to die from a heart attack than those physically fit.
Dr. Lars Ekelund, Duke University Medical Center

My routine for fighting the travel "blahs" is to eat a light dinner, preferably only fish and vegetables, and get up an hour early in the morning to jog. If it is too dark outside, I run in place in my room. In effect, I trade off a little extra sleep for the good feeling and added stamina that comes from regular exercise.

If you want to adopt a physical fitness program, it is strongly recommended that you consult your physician prior to beginning. This is of particular importance if you are over forty years old.

Exercise gives you stamina, energy, and vitality.

There are several other rules about exercising that should be adhered to:

1. **Warm up prior to beginning strenuous exercise.** One of the best ways to do so is to perform a

limited number of stretching exercises. There are several excellent books on the market that can tell you the best ways to stretch and thereby avoid pulling muscles.

2. **Start slowly and gradually work up to extended activity.** For example, if you decide to start jogging, your first two weeks should be devoted to alternating between short periods of jogging and walking.

3. **After exercising, take at least ten minutes to slowly cool off and stretch out again.** This is the minimum time required to do so. People in a hurry often forget this important advice by taking a cold shower immediately after exercising. They fail to realize that their heart is already stressed by increased blood pressure and the production of a hormone called epinephrine that occurs when you cease vigorous activity. The cold shower can cause further stimulation of the heart resulting in a potentially dangerous condition.[16]

If you are not too tired, the best time to exercise is at the end of your workday. This is an excellent way to put the stress of the day behind you. It will also aid sleep. The one negative aspect of exercising in the evening is that it may stimulate your appetite. A heavy meal is not recommended because your body does not have sufficient time to burn off the calories before you go to bed.

One additional point about exercising: If you do not enjoy it and view it as just another chore, it could be harmful. According to Dr. Kenneth Greenspan: "Exercising while under stress can be dangerous because it puts an extra load on your heart." [17]

Other good health directives to follow include:
- Do not smoke,
- Keep your weight down, and

A man too busy to take care of his health is like a mechanic too busy to take care of his tools.

Spanish Proverb

• Minimize the amount of fat consumed in your diet.

Fatty foods, such as meat, eggs, cheese, and ice cream contain high levels of cholesterol. Overwhelming evidence supports the theory that cholesterol is an important factor in heart ailments and cancer. According to the National Center for Health Statistics, these illnesses account for nearly 50 percent of the deaths in the United States.

A study of 356,000 men, age thirty-five to fifty-seven, found that 80 percent had cholesterol levels over the recommended level of 200 milligrams per deciliter of blood. The heart attack rate climbs sharply above the 200 level.[18] The heart attack rate for the forty to forty-four age group with the 200 level was twice that for those with levels below 182.[19] Dr. Jeremiah Stamler noted the importance of this discovery: "The claim is incorrect that excess risk does not start until the cholesterol reaches a markedly elevated level."[20]

According to the American Cancer Society, the best defense against cancer is to eat less fat and eat more fiber. Dr. Albert Mendeloff, a Johns Hopkins University gastrointestinal expert, recommends an intake of 30 to 60 grams per day of high fiber foods such as bran cereal, fresh vegetables, and fruits. Do not go overboard on fiber, Mendeloff warns, because enormously high consumption of fiber may lead to excessive loss of some trace minerals.

A long-term, steady diet of foods containing beta-carotene (i.e., carrots, tomatoes, spinach, asparagus, and cantaloupe) is now considered helpful in inhibiting cancer. Vegetables like cabbage, broccoli, cauliflower, and brussels sprouts are packed with cancer-fighters called phyto-chemicals.

If you decide to change your eating habits for the better, don't try to do it abruptly. The trick is to gradually make changes so your body can adjust slowly. The best approach is to change only a few meals each week. In a relatively short time period you'll have a healthy diet and will be enjoying it too.

So far I've outlined two of the most important health habits: getting regular exercise and maintaining a low-fat diet. Several additional good health practices include:

1. **Keep regular sleep habits.** What counts is both the regularity of sleeping patterns and the amount. Altering sleeping patterns frequently creates the feeling of always being tired and lowers resistance to colds and flu.

Do you occasionally have problems falling asleep at night? If so, you are in good company, as more than one-third of the population has insomnia from time to time. Studies show that missing an hour or two of normal sleep for a night or two does not affect your overall performance at work.[21] This is because the human body can develop tolerance for sleep loss. Therefore, do not worry about getting to sleep quickly the night before a big meeting or an important presentation. Chronic sleep deprivation, however, is a serious matter. Studies have shown that people who regularly fail to get enough sleep are less resistant to disease, more accident prone, and less able to starve off stress.

There are several effective techniques for overcoming insomnia. It is senseless to continue tossing and turning. Worrying about wakefulness only makes things worse. Instead, read a few chapters of a novel or get out of bed and perform some routine task such as straightening up your closet. Similarly, you can work on some aspect of a hobby that does not require a lot of thought.

Insomnia is most prevalent on Sunday night when most people are well rested from the weekend. In "On Getting a Good Night's Sleep," Dr. Leonard Hayflick noted, "The shorter the time between waking up from one night's sleep and going to sleep again, the more difficult it will be to get to sleep." People who do not work on weekends often sleep a couple of extra hours past their weekday alarm. By Sunday night their body clocks are readjusted to a pattern different from that during the week.

If you maintain the same sleep patterns during workdays and on days off, waking at the same time and avoiding an afternoon nap, you can arrive at work fresh and ready to take on the events of the week.

There are several other techniques for preventing insomnia:

- Exercise regularly, but no later than three hours before bedtime.
- Avoid daytime naps.
- Do not use alcohol as a "nightcap."
- Think positive thoughts before going to bed.
- Do not drink beverages containing caffeine after 6 p.m.

2. **Minimize your intake of caffeine-loaded drinks like coffee, tea, and colas.** Growing medical evidence suggests that excessive consumption of caffeine may be a contributor to such diseases as ulcers and cancer. A study at Stanford University indicated that middle-aged men who consumed three or more cups of coffee a day had high levels of LDL cholesterol in their blood—the type that is linked to heart disease.[22]

The bottom line is that by modifying your eating, drinking, and exercise habits, and eliminating tobacco products, you substantially reduce the risk of serious disease. Possibly the major payoff from maintaining good health habits is that you will experience the joy of being physically fit. With this good feeling comes increased stamina and enthusiasm—key ingredients for success as a leader.

One final note about maintaining good health habits—be careful that your pursuit of health does not become an obsession. You could become a health addict. As with everything, moderation is the key.

C. FIND WAYS TO RELEASE TENSION AND ENJOY YOURSELF

You need to reduce stress both at work and at home. No one can continuously perform at top speed when under excessive stress; it will eventually affect one's health. Your ability to achieve over the long term is enhanced by adopting various coping strategies that can be applied on the job.

1. **In everything you undertake give it your best.** I have never had regrets when I have done so. It is only when I did not properly prepare for a meeting or did not adequately address the issues in a report that I felt badly. Unquestionably, you feel your best when you do your best. Even making the extra effort will make you feel like a new person.
2. **Avoid the tendency to take on more than you can properly handle.** This is a particular problem for the small percentage of the population (approximately 15–20 percent) that are high achievers. Most leaders are in this category.

Slow down!

If you keep burning the candle at both ends, there won't be any candle.
J. W. "Bill" Marriott, Jr.,
USA TODAY

To avoid burnout you should make a conscious decision to pace your days more evenly and to concentrate on only a few major areas or projects at a time. Deepak Chopra calls this "doing more by doing less." Therefore, build some slack into your day so you have time to reflect on the key issues facing you. I would much rather have team members achieve major improvement in a limited number of areas rather than a little improvement in all of them. The idea is to get one or two items under control, then go on to two more. There is nothing more nerve-racking than trying to do too much at once. I have actually seen it make people ill.

There is one exception to my recommendation of not overloading yourself with work. If your present job has become stressful, if it no longer provides sufficient challenge or rewards, it may be helpful to tackle a new assignment (such as a special project) that can be done after normal work hours. You may even want to turn a hobby into a part-time business. If this additional work is stimulating, it can actually reduce the stress you previously felt. Many people find such an approach energizing.

Excessive hours are not a problem if they contribute to your personal growth and a feeling that you are in control of your destiny. This is why many entrepreneurs can work day and night and with very little stress.

3. **Whenever possible, relax during lunch.** Try to work out, take a walk, sit in the park, visit an art gallery, or browse around a department store. One of my friends in the banking business makes it a practice to take a mid-day break to run several miles. He maintains that the workout eliminates built-up tension, thus enabling him to work long hours without getting tired. Whenever you need a break, eat lunch alone in a peaceful environment.

Get your mind off business by reading a book or magazine. When you return to work, you will feel refreshed—ready to take on new challenges.

Avoid regularly eating a hurried lunch on the job. Gulping down your food surrounded by all the problems and tensions of the day can be detrimental to your health. Some doctors claim that cholesterol levels increase substantially when a person eats while under stress.[23]

4. **Take time to relax.** Occasionally seek out a moment of solitude, and let your voice mail catch your calls. Let your mind wander away from business matters by visualizing a quiet, peaceful scene. Imagine a beautiful sunset in the mountains, a grassy windswept bluff, or the silvery light of the moon upon a still lake. During such quiet periods the heartbeat slows and the blood pressure falls. The brain, which controls the body, refocuses from something unpleasant and stressful to something pleasant, and the body responds accordingly.

One quick way to release stress on or off the job is to breathe deeply and consciously. Although you may not realize it, tense situations cause you to breathe more shallowly. By taking several intentional, deep breaths, you can cause a remarkable change in how you feel.[24]

5. **Seek jobs that you enjoy.** Our time on earth is too short to constantly toil at things we really do not like to do. That does not mean that you should drop everything and go live on a tropical island. Yet, you should periodically evaluate whether you are devoting your work life to a goal that you feel good about or one that you will someday regret. Looking at your situation from this perspective is the first and most important step in making career decisions.

People rarely succeed in life unless they have fun doing it.
Bits and Pieces
May, 1985

6. **Try to view change as an opportunity to learn new things and develop yourself rather than as a threat.** There will always be events in our lives that we do not like. Changes will keep occurring no matter what we do to resist them. One of the keys to managing stress is learning to use the changes life presents as a new beginning to grow in terms of your values and spirit. Dr. Bernie S. Siegel, author of many popular books, says: "Finding your true self and the way in which you want to love the world is really what your journey is all about."[25] Change viewed in a positive way facilitates this journey because it opens up new developmental opportunities.

7. **Make "to do" lists.** Possibly the most effective stress management technique I have utilized over the years is to make lists of things I need to accomplish. I keep a list of "to do" items on my desk at work and another on my bedroom dresser. Once I place an item on a list, I feel freed of trying to remember it and worrying about it. Before I go to bed at night, I clear my mind by jotting down all the action items I can think of for the next day. This helps me have a restful sleep.

Leaders need to understand that not every problem has to be solved today, nor does every task have to be accomplished before you leave the office.

Did you ever hear of someone on his deathbed saying "I wish I'd spent more time at the office?"

Over the years my efforts to clean everything up before I go home at night have led to considerable stress. I learned that it is often more productive to stop work when I am tired and return to the office earlier than usual the next morning. When you are fresh, you can accomplish far more in a shorter time period.

D. LEARN HOW TO RELAX AND ENJOY YOUR FREE TIME.

Professor William Theobald of Purdue University has been researching the leisure patterns of leaders for years. After surveying sixty chief executive officers, he found that 60 percent of them did not normally take vacations. Of those who did, 40 percent cut them short.[26] These figures substantiate the widely held belief that achievement-oriented people simply have a hard time letting down and relaxing. "These individuals tend to view leisure time as unproductive. . .They really don't enjoy it," says Prof. Theobald.[27]

As their careers reach the sunset phase, usually after age sixty, many hard-charging business leaders reach the conclusion that they have paid too steep a price for their success. Having lived in a "pressure-cooker" for so long, their health often fails prematurely. With high blood pressure or a heart ailment, they are unable to fully enjoy the fruits of their labors. Often I have heard such people say, "If only I had relaxed a little more along the way," or "If I just hadn't put myself under such strain all the time."

Half the battle in fighting stress is to have more fun in life.

Fortunately, it is not too late to change your lifestyle. You can find a better **balance** between work and relaxation. You do not have to go to the other extreme and neglect your career. Continue working hard, but decide that your personal time is going to be more relaxing and enjoyable. Aristotle extolled the philosophy of living a balanced life when he observed that all vice stems from either an excess or a deficiency of a virtue.[28]

There are many ways to relax and enjoy your time off. Here are a few that have been successfully used by business leaders:

Be still and know!

1. **Devote twenty to thirty minutes a day to meditation and prayer.** Select a place where you can be alone. A peaceful, quiet setting is best. This

time should be yours and yours alone without feeling a need to justify it to anyone. Let your mind roam at will. Give praise. Think about the good things in your life—your loved ones, your past successes, and your dreams for the future. Come to terms with the mistakes you made. **Be at peace with yourself, for you are a unique person with much to contribute to this world.**

My preferred prayerful quiet time is the early morning. I usually spend a half-hour or so observing the sunrise as I jog. What an uplifting way to begin the day!

2. **Connect to nature.** Jogging at sunrise is uplifting because it connects me with forces in nature that are far stronger than myself. Gardening, canoeing on a still lake, and walking in a snowy forest have the same effect. Such quiet time in nature helps put my daily burdens in proper perspective.

3. **Develop some interests outside of business to help you get your mind off work.** The best way to do so is to be inquisitive about other matters. Make it a practice to notice new things each day, whether it is in people, nature, or the works of man. Besides enjoying the outdoors with all its fascinating colors and changes, I like to observe the construction of new buildings. To me, it is exciting to witness something permanent being created where there was nothing before.

The surest way not to become tired is to lose yourself in something in which you have a profound conviction.
Dr. Norman Vincent Peale
The Power of Positive Thinking

Involving yourself with hobbies is an excellent way to accomplish the objective of eliminating worry. Fishing, playing tennis, golfing, collecting stamps, painting, learning, and chatting on the Internet all accomplish the same thing: they keep your attention. Such activities, even though they can be quite demanding, seldom produce stress. This is because you elect to do them, and you can moderate your participation level.

Everyone needs a hobby outside of work that is totally immersing, rewarding, and pleasurable. John Wanamaker, founder of the famous Philadelphia department store, said, "People who cannot find time for recreation are obligated sooner or later to find time for illness."

Your best career move may be to lighten up and become easier to like.

4. **Develop a sense of humor.** A good sense of humor not only relieves stress, but it also helps your career. It has been my experience that promotions usually go to people who are competent **and** liked. One of the best ways to be liked is to not take yourself too seriously. You should be able to poke fun at yourself and enjoy a good joke. People who are dry, stiff, and humorless are at a serious disadvantage in competing for bigger assignments.

In the intense world of the leader, humor plays an important role. First, it helps team members relate to their managers and vice versa. Second, humor relieves tension that may be impeding clear thinking. Many times I have heard a funny remark or joke made at an appropriate time in a meeting defuse an ugly debate or bring focus to an unproductive discussion. Finally, laughter is good for our emotional and physical health. In his book *Anatomy of an Illness,* Norman Cousins goes further. He says, "laughter helps to muster the energy needed to combat disease."

The sharing of a good joke with someone or laughing at life's absurdities can make almost any situation bearable. Humor, however, should never be at the expense of someone else. *Racial, ethnic, religious, or sexist jokes have no place in the life of a leader who cares about the dignity of others.*

Worry, not hard work, is what drains energy and vitality.

5. **Keep your mind on the pleasant aspects of life** such as fond memories, the beauty around you, the joy of sharing and giving to others, and the moments spent with loved ones. Try to forget the

painful or ugly events of life that lead to stress. Instead, focus on what is good, what is right, and what is beautiful.

6. **Concentrate your energies on matters that you can have a positive influence on.** Many of us dissipate our energy by trying to change or improve things we have no control over. It is of little value to keep striving with all your might for some unattainable degree of success. Well-adjusted people are able to differentiate between the elements that they can control and those that they cannot. They focus on achieving the possible.

7. **Maintain your self-confidence.** When you feel down or slightly depressed about a recent failure, stop and take stock of your past achievements. The realization that you have had major successes in the past and that the future is always open should help you regain your self-confidence. **If you succeeded once, you can always do it again.**

    It is my observation that the true winners in life have something going for them beyond being at the right place at the right time: they view life from a long-term perspective. Winners fully expect to be successful eventually. There may be setbacks along the way, but they are merely short detours to be corrected and learned from.

8. **Do not try to be the "parent" of everything.** Many leaders I know place undue stress upon themselves by thinking that they have to be responsible for everything at work and at home. They also feel obligated to actively support important community and charitable activities.

    When you feel overwhelmed by obligations, stop and sort out your "have to's" from your "choose to's." More often than not, you will find that you really do not have to do many things; you **choose** to do them. Begin the process of simplifying your

Yesterday is experience, Tomorrow is hope.[29]

Simplify your life!

life by saying "no" more often to demands on your personal time. Delegate more responsibility to your team members and family members. And finally, as much as possible, pay others to perform services for you, such as cleaning, cutting the grass, raking the leaves, and shoveling the snow. I have found that a simple, private lifestyle that centers on my family helps regenerate my "batteries."

9. **Realize that you do not have to obtain perfection in everything you do.** Perfectionists are particularly prone to stress because they are easily disturbed if everything is not just right. They also tend to worry about how well they performed in the past. "If I had just done . . ." is a common statement from such people.

Learn to walk away from unfinished tasks that can wait until tomorrow. I will never forget working with my father-in-law, Don Harrison, fixing his farm fence in Hanover, Pennsylvania. One summer night at dusk we had nearly completed the repairs. I asked, "Do you want to keep going and finish the job?" His answer: "Let's go relax; it will be here tomorrow." Being able to occasionally say, "It will wait" or "So what" is necessary to avoid building undue pressure on yourself.

10. **Be playful. Lighten up. Have fun.** The normal person living to age 78 has 683,280 hours of life. This is too long a period not to have fun. Therefore, enjoy the small pleasures of life. Periodically do something spontaneous that comes from your heart. Once when my wife was on a business trip, I went out of my way to locate her car at the airport so I could put a note on the windshield telling her "I love you." You can send an unexpected gift to a spouse or friend, arrange a surprise birthday or anniversary party for a relative, or take a box of doughnuts into the office.

11. **Develop the spiritual side of your life.** The spiritual side of your life is just as important as the physical side. Just as your body will atrophy over time unless you eat right, get plenty of sleep, and exercise; so will your spirit become dormant unless you frequently think of others, meditate, and pray.

Sir John Templeton, the renowned financier and philanthropist said, "True success in life is possible only if you've made the business of living a spiritually richer and happier experience.[30]

Focusing on your spiritual development frees you from the prison of being preoccupied with your own problems and ailments. It opens you to become sympathetic to the problems of society and to seek ways to serve mankind.

One of the best ways to "free your spirit" is regularly attending religious services to meditate and pray. In addition, frequently do things for others. Dennis Waitley says, "Call, visit, or write someone in need every day of your life. Demonstrate your faith by passing it on to others."[31]

There are many ways of managing stress both on and off the job. You need to figure out which of these suggestions are appropriate for you. The best overall advice I've ever come across is captured in the essence of a single Hebrew word "dayenu", or "it is enough." "To live dayenu as a way of life is to **be ready to embrace the mystery of each moment fully and then let it go.**"[32]

"For where your treasure is, there will your heart be also"

Matthew 6:21

VII

Striving for a More Satisfying Personal Life

No man can deliver the goods if his heart is heavier than the load.

  Frank Irving Fletcher

If your ambition in life is to reach your highest leadership potential, it is a definite advantage to have a supportive and happy personal life. With all the stress and strain leaders face each day, they cannot afford to be preoccupied with ongoing, serious personal problems. A troubled marriage, serious financial difficulties, and problems with children and relatives drain valuable emotional energy away from the all-out effort required to lead others successfully. On the other hand, a loving, supportive home environment can help you relax and "refuel" for the next challenge at work.

Obviously, everyone is going to have personal problems from time to time. The ability to cope with them is dependent on the individual's spiritual strength and the help and comfort obtained from friends and loved ones.

Having a satisfying personal life is a major determinant of long-term job success. *U.S. News and World Report* published the findings of a study of one million "ordinary millionaires"—those people who had principally made their fortunes on their own, not by inheritance. The article points out that the vast majority of them attribute much of their success to a stable and satisfying home life.

The purpose of this chapter is to assist you in maximizing your long-term leadership effectiveness by providing ideas and suggestions for ensuring a more satisfying personal life.

If one advances confidently in the direction of his dreams, and endeavors to live the life which he has imagined, he will meet with success unexpected in common hours.

  Henry David Thoreau

1. **Develop a well-formulated statement of purpose or mission** in your life. Preoccupied with work and busy with their families, most people only have a vague idea of what they ultimately want in life. For years I too focused on short-term personal objectives, such as obtaining another degree or getting the next promotion. All this changed when our church adult class participated in an unusual

exercise. We were asked to spend fifteen quiet minutes visualizing what we wanted written as an epitaph on our tombstone. The exercise forced me to think of what I wanted to be remembered for after spending seventy to eighty years on earth. This was a difficult exercise because I had not given much thought to the true meaning of life or how I could contribute to making it better for others.

By reflecting upon what I valued most, I developed the following mission statement for my life:

> *To help others reach their highest leadership potential by sharing my knowledge, skills, and values through coaching, teaching, writing, and by the example I set.*

How uplifting it was to decide on this mission and set out on the journey of fulfilling it!

Great men and women have a purpose or mission in life that is related in one form or another to giving themselves to others. Mohandas Gandhi, Albert Schweitzer, Mother Teresa, Martin Luther King, Jr., and Madame Curie devoted their lives to eliminating suffering and improving living conditions for all people.

Success, therefore, should not be measured by one's power, status, or fame. Rather, it should be measured by how much one gives of himself or herself to make this earth a little better for others. It is only when an individual's mission or purpose is focused outwardly on others that he or she can be at peace. **Success then becomes being at peace with yourself.**

Since your work and personal life change over time, you should periodically review your mission

Cultivate optimism by committing yourself to a cause, a plan, or a value system. You'll feel that you are growing in a meaningful direction which will help you rise above day-to-day setbacks.[1]
Dr. Robert Conroy

statement to determine if it accurately reflects your current desires for the future. It is possible that you will want to revise or change your mission several times in your lifetime. What is appropriate at age twenty-five may not be at forty-five or sixty.

For your mission to become reality it must be accompanied by **specific goals**. A good time to establish personal goals is at the beginning of each new year. With the holidays behind you and most businesses in a lull, this is an excellent time to reflect on what you want to accomplish during the coming year.

A well thought out mission statement and specific goals are of little value unless accompanied by **self-discipline**. To achieve what you want in life you must work relentlessly and systematically toward your objective without being sidetracked.

2. **Add some variety to your life.** How easy it is to get into a comfortable routine of doing the same things, the same way, day after day! A certain amount of routine has its value, but too much routine can lead to boredom, complacency, and sadness.

According to the research performed by Dr. Diane Tice, a psychologist at Case Western University: "The single most popular way to shake sadness is to turn to the company of others."[2] The following United Technologies Corporation advertisement that appeared in the *Wall Street Journal* provides some additional advice on how to overcome the "blues" by introducing variety and spice to your life.

"Get Out of That Rut"

Oscar Wilde said,
"Consistency is
the last refuge of
the unimaginative."
So stop getting up
at 6:05.
Get up at 5:06.
Walk a mile at dawn.
Find a new way
to drive to work.
Switch chores with
your spouse
next Saturday.
Buy a wok.
Study wildflowers.
Stay up alone all night.
Read to the blind.
Start counting
brown-eyed blondes
or blondes.
Subscribe to an
out-of-town paper.
Canoe at midnight.
Don't write to your
congressman;
take a whole scout
troop to see him.
Learn to speak
Italian.
Teach some kid
the thing you do best.
Listen to two hours of
uninterrupted Mozart.
Take up aerobic dancing.
Leap out of that rut.

**Savor life.
Remember, we only
pass this way once."**

Human beings, especially high achievers, are much like plants—every four or five years they need to be repotted or regenerated by taking on a significant new career challenge. This could be a promotion or a lateral transfer to a different position. If your present employer is unwilling to provide such opportunities and you are not prepared to go elsewhere, rededicate yourself to making the best of your present job. In addition, try to take on a challenging after-work activity in your community. Head a charity funds drive, or become an officer in a civic or social club. Other people obtain self-actualization by turning a hobby into a part-time business or seeking a graduate degree.

You should never stand still in life. Keep growing and developing!

3. **Seek a mate for life that is a buddy or a best friend** —someone to whom you can say, "I love you for what you are and how you make me feel." I am blessed in this situation with my wife, Donna. We enjoy being together and care a great deal for each other.

To me, there are two critical requirements for a successful marriage. The first is that your top priority in terms of time and attention must go towards building and maintaining a strong relationship with your partner. Everything else—your children, career, and hobbies—must be secondary. Second, there must be a high degree of mutual trust between the partners. Being faithful to each other over the years is the foundation of this trust.

Donna Hulsizer, Ed.D., at Harvard University, adds two more ingredients for a successful mar-

Communicating frequently and intimately is the best prescription for a successful marriage.[3]
Dr. Howard Markman, Ph.D.

A relationship is a living thing. It needs and benefits from the same attention to detail that an artist lavishes on his art.[4]

riage: "Both spouses should talk openly about their feelings, and each should have a substantial interest outside the home.[5] This provides self-esteem that is essential for a relationship to work.

One final thought about marriage: think of your relationship as a partnership in which you both share in the affairs of the home. This means that both partners should be willing to help with all household chores and to care for the children.

4. **Take time to smell the daisies**. By this, I mean spend some time during your "helter skelter" career to sense and appreciate the beauty, emotions, and excitement of the small things in life—such as quietly observing a robin feeding her young, walking in a snowy forest, watching children at play, or participating in pleasant conversation with family or friends. To fully enjoy such pleasures you need to periodically slow down and open your heart and senses to what is occurring around you. Drink it in with the same gusto that you display at work.

Rabbi Alexander M. Schindler, President of the Union of American Hebrew Congregations, advises leaders to "never be too busy for the wonder and awe of life. Be reverent for each dawning day. Embrace each hour. Seize each golden moment."[6]

Carlyle was right when he said, "this life is only a gleam of light between two eternities." And still some folks take it so hectically and so seriously.

Amos Parrish

Enjoying the small pleasures of life is easier said than done for intense leaders who are used to a frantic pace, but it is vitally important that you do so before it is too late. In time your health may fail, and you will not have the ability to enjoy life as you may want to.

For the first few years after graduating from college, I was caught up in the typical syndrome of working nearly every waking hour. Had I known then what I know now, I would have tried harder to relax and spend more time with my family and friends.

I was frequently away on business and chose to do office work evenings and weekends. Thankfully, before it was too late, I realized what was happening and decided to make some changes in my lifestyle. I quit bringing work home unless it was absolutely necessary. I started making more time for my children; I attended their school events whenever possible and did things with them on the weekends. I made it a policy to never run an errand without some company. Each Saturday I took one of my sons or my daughter to lunch. I drove them to school. Occasionally, one of the children accompanied me on a business trip. These times together made me feel a part of their lives. Best of all, it provided all of us with many fond memories.

Build your "memory bank" now before it is too late to make deposits.

It took a while, but I finally realized what is truly important in life. It is not making more and more money, but loving those close to you and enjoying them while you can. As Henry Ward Beecher said, "No man can tell whether he is rich or poor by turning to his ledger. It is the heart that makes a man rich. He is rich according to what he is, not according to what he has."

Once in a while it is refreshing to take a personal day off to go to a ballgame, see your kids in a play at school, be with friends, or just relax at home. This does not mean that you stop working hard or reduce your regular office hours. Rather, it means taking a little time off now and then for the important people in your life.

Disconnect periodically so you can recharge.
Steven Berglas,
Psychologist,
Harvard Medical
School

It should be your personal policy to take all your allotted vacation time. In my career I have never seen anyone rewarded for skipping vacations. Leaders need periods of total rest to maintain their health, reflect on their lives, and enjoy their families. Forgetting about work for an extended period has the added benefit of enabling the individual to return to work with renewed energy and creativity.

Skipping vacations could be a sign of insecurity. What is the individual afraid will be discovered during his absence? The leader's personnel also need some breathing space—to occasionally be free of their boss. Vacations are good for everyone: the leader, the team, and the company.

5. **At home, put building relationships ahead of task completion**. All their lives leaders have been trained to get out the work, to accomplish more and more. Often they carry this attitude home and become preoccupied with accomplishing chores and fix-up projects evenings and weekends. Worse yet, they bring home their notebook computer to review and send E-mail.

Most leaders, to one degree or another, have over-commitment problems. The responsibility for running an organization just does not cease the moment you leave the office. Important problems have to be dealt with as they occur, no matter how long they take.

*When you're gone, your children will **not** remember all the recognition and promotions you achieved at work. They will only remember the time you did or did not spend with them.*

The solution to the challenge of balancing task completion with building relationships at home is not to simply say: "Stop bringing home your work." Instead, you should devise ways to clearly separate family time from work time when you are home.

The most important family time is just before dinner, during dinner, and after dinner. This two-hour block of time should be dedicated to family time and family time alone. During this period, do not even get close to your "to do" list or your computer. Instead, hang around your family. Become involved in what your spouse and kids did during the day. Be sensitive to their concerns and

170

problems. If you must do office work or pay the bills, do it after the children start their homework or after they go to bed. Better yet, devote the entire evening to the family and get up an hour earlier in the morning to work while the house is quiet. You can get more accomplished this way, and, best of all, you will not lose out on any precious family time.

6. **Keep in shape physically and mentally**. It is important to keep healthy; that is why I run several miles each day, eat the right foods, and get plenty of rest. One of the things I enjoy most in life is rising early and jogging in the splendor of the morning sunrise. At that time I feel very close to God. When I return home, I feel like a totally different person. I am at peace with myself and feel an incredible lift in energy.

Your health must come first. Without it, you have nothing.

It is surprising how much more effective you can be on the job if you feel healthy. You are more alert, energetic, and pleasant.

7. **Give something of yourself to others both on and off the job**. Some leaders act as if their lives have two compartments—one for work and one for their personal lives. At home with family and friends they are empathetic and caring; but at work they become insensitive and self-centered. With this metamorphosis they lose a wonderful opportunity to be God's person in a setting that cries out for love.

Loving is the only sure road out of darkness, the only serum known that cures self-centeredness.

Ron McKuen

The great paradox of life is that the more you give of yourself, the more you receive. Deepak Chopra adds: "If you want understanding, give it. If you want respect, give it. If you want love, give it."

8. **Do not risk more financially than you can afford to lose**. A man or woman preoccupied with risky investments is surely not going to have his or her mind on the job. The temptation is to seek the high

returns normally associated with risky investments. Unfortunately, you always hear about the few who succeeded with this strategy but seldom about the many who failed.

Your policy should always be never to gamble the future of your family for the sake of making it big financially. Years ago, Donna and I made the decision that we would first accrue sufficient funds for our children's college education before making any other investments. What peace of mind this has provided us over the years!

My investment strategy has three basic components. First, I always look for **quality** in investment opportunities. Investing in the best costs more initially, but it usually pays off with higher returns in the long run. Second, I **diversify** my savings by investing in various types of financial and tangible assets. Examples of financial assets include stocks, bonds, and money market funds. Some of the most popular tangible assets are real estate and precious metals. By not putting all my eggs in one basket, I average out the effects of inflationary and deflationary periods.

The world is just too complicated, dynamic, and changeable for one to be an expert in all matters that affect the value of investments. Even professional mutual funds managers cannot consistently predict the direction of the markets. Individual investors have even less chance to do so. Therefore, the best policy is to be a steady, long-term investor and keep diversified with a sizable percentage of savings in conservative investments.

A word of advice for those who have stock option or stock savings plans with their companies. Even though it might be attractive to make heavy investments in your company's shares, be careful not to overdo it. Over the years I've seen too many people burned by following such a strategy. There are just too many unforeseen developments that can permanently depress the value of a company's stock. Diversification, once again, should be your primary investment strategy. Therefore, put no more than 20 percent of your total savings in your company's stock.

The third part of my investment strategy is to seek a **reasonable**, not excessive, rate of return from investments. I believe that financial success in most cases comes from not being greedy. Remember that all hogs eventually get slaughtered!

9. **Start early in your career to put away a little money from each paycheck** into an emergency fund or what I call a "safety net." As with everything in life, your career is bound to have a number of peaks and valleys. Nothing is more depressing than absolute financial dependency on your employer; then you can never afford to quit or change careers. Your objective should be to save enough so that by the time you are at mid-career, you can live for a year or two without a job.

The habit of saving is itself an education, it fosters every virtue, teaches self-denial and cultivates a sense of order.

T. T. Munger

Having a sizable nest egg by your mid-forties is no longer a nice thing to do; it is a necessity. It is the middle-level management group, primarily people in their forties, that is most susceptible to layoffs due to mergers, recessions, and corporate restructuring.

The economic hardships on unemployed middle-aged people are severe. By age forty-five most couples have upscaled their standard of living by taking on substantial new debt to purchase larger homes and more expensive cars. On top of this, their children are just entering college, and their

Career job protection can no longer be guaranteed by any employer.

newly retired parents often need financial assistance.

As one displaced airline engineering manager bitterly told me: "After twenty-five years of dedicated service, I can't believe what happened. All of a sudden I'm dispensable. I always thought that if you worked hard and were loyal, that you'd be taken care of." Lulled into a feeling that his company would provide for him for life, this man had failed to prepare for his rainy day.

Besides the specter of increased layoffs for middle managers, there is another development that makes life-long saving crucial: the trend toward reduction or elimination of retirement benefits by financially troubled corporations. This is something that rarely happened before. In the past, one could retire with the assurance that benefits would continue until death.

The handwriting is on the wall! The paternalistic days of the corporate world are gone forever. **There is no job security!** As a young person in the business world today, you can no longer think of a forty-five-year career with a single company—even if you are an outstanding performer. A time span of ten to fifteen years is more realistic—if the company remains profitable.

Only three out of every one hundred people reach retirement with a reasonable degree of financial security.
U. S. Dept. of Labor[7]

Most young people in the work force live on thin margins. Often, dangerously in debt, they have no cushion available for an emergency and little saved for retirement. Even though they realize that Social Security will be unable to meet their retirement needs, they continue spending as if there were no tomorrow, hoping somehow that the future will take care of itself.

My advice to people in their 20's and 30's is to accumulate savings equal to one year's salary as soon as possible and thereafter save at least 10 percent of all earnings. This level of savings should be sufficient to finance a comfortable retirement. If you wait until you are in your 40's to get started, you will have to double the savings rate to nearly 20 percent.

I do not know how many times my father told me that you can be more valuable to your company and sleep better at night if you have the confidence of knowing that you **can** quit. You do not want to be pressured into compromising your closely held values for the sake of meeting house payments. Therefore, develop the habit of saving regularly. Sooner or later you'll be glad you did.

The doors are open to a better life! The future is open. It all depends on your attitude and outlook. You can choose to rush through life on the way to the grave, or you can choose to slow down a bit and take more time to enjoy your family and friends. You can choose to be grumpy, hard, and dull, or you can choose to be happy, warm, and interesting. **The possibilities of making your life more loving, interesting, and fulfilling are almost limitless.**

Before you turn your attention to the concept of lifetime learning and how best to develop your leadership skills, I would like to leave you with a powerful thought about seeking happiness:

> **Happiness cannot be traveled to, owned, earned, worn, or consumed. Happiness is the spiritual experience of living every minute with love, grace, and gratitude.**[8]

Today is the beginning of the rest of your life.
Author Unknown

VIII

Leadership Self-Development
—A Lifetime Pursuit

Leadership development is a lifetime journey—not a brief trip.

Successful leaders recognize that developing and maintaining their leadership skills is a lifetime pursuit. In their study of ninety top leaders in all fields, Bennis and Nanus found, "It is the capacity to develop and improve their skills that distinguishes leaders from their followers."[1] The researchers also came to the conclusion that "leaders are perpetual learners."[2] Their nature is to be curious about learning new things— asking frequent questions and probing for understanding. Once they learn something they internalize it so that it remains in their "memory bank" until needed in the future.

No matter what level you have achieved in your career, you cannot afford to become static. All too often, leaders reach a certain plateau in their organizations and then begin to coast. They lose the will to fight for what they believe in. Simultaneously, the nature and scope of their operations continue to change, leaving them obsolete in terms of knowledge and skills. According to Jeffrey Schmidt, a managing director at Towers Perrin, "You have to assume that the half-life of the skill set you've got is about three to five years."[3]

The people who succeed are those who have the self-discipline to develop themselves.

Think of how enthusiastic and energetic you were to acquire new job knowledge when you first began your management career. More than likely, you were like a sponge—learning everything you could as quickly as possible. You probably took stacks of industry studies and trade journals home each night and studied them diligently.

If you truly want to reach your highest potential as a leader, it is imperative that you continue this almost child-like zest for learning throughout your career.

Three powerful forces that are currently shaping the business world cause the need for continuous self-development. First, due to global communications systems like the Internet being readily available to everyone, the extent of knowledge is exploding at an

ever-increasing rate. New management and techno-
logical concepts can now be disseminated to millions
of people in seconds at very little cost. In the past it
took weeks or even months to print and distribute
journals and books. Second, global commerce is
becoming commonplace, even for small businesses.
Success in the global arena requires more than just a
good product line; it requires a detailed knowledge of
the customs and values of different cultures.

The third force shaping the business world is the
rapid change in how work is organized and performed.
Fortune magazine calls this phenomenon "a social
transformation as massive and wrenching as the
industrial revolution."[4] Frequent restructuring and
downsizing is the norm, even for healthy companies.
Layers of middle management continue to be
eliminated. New forms of organization keep emerging
with variations of leaderless groups and cross-
functional teams. The result is less and less dependency on traditional hierarchical reporting relationships. Managers are required to move easily from
one function to another, successfully integrating
diverse disciplines.[6]

The bottom line is that you can never afford to become complacent in terms of your knowledge and
skills. When you reach the point that you feel you
know all there is to know, watch out, for it won't be
long until you're replaced by someone who has made
the investment in time and energy to keep up-to-date.

At first the reader might think that being a lifetime
learner must occur at the expense of having an enjoyable personal life. Quite the contrary, my wife and I
consider learning a hobby. We enjoy reading together,
often sitting for hours studying and discussing topics
and issues in the field of business.

Years ago I decided that the normal reading of management journals was insufficient for my own growth
and development. I wanted to develop as rapidly as

"A portfolio of up-to-date skills is your best guarantee of work now and in the future."[5]

Unless you try to do something be-yond what you already mastered you will never grow.
Ronald Osborn

possible. What was needed was a series of learning experiences that involved a **commitment** on my part to others.

My first major developmental effort that required a commitment to others was to obtain an MBA degree at night and then to undertake an MS degree in finance. In both cases, I had to request tuition aid approval from my manager and submit grades to him at the end of each semester. Next, I taught MBA courses part-time. Realizing that the students paid hard-earned dollars for the courses, I felt obligated to do the best teaching job possible. Several years later I began writing articles for management and training journals and taught leadership seminars at work. Writing this book has been my latest learning experience. All of these activities involved strong commitments on my part to people, thereby accelerating my development beyond what it would have been otherwise.

Contrast this type of commitment to one that you keep to yourself, say a resolution to learn more about leadership by reading a book a month. How many resolutions of this type are kept?

For maximum benefit and effectiveness, the commitments you make to grow and develop must be well thought out and organized. This requires that you:

"You got to have a dream. If you don't have a dream, how you gonna make a dream come true?"
South Pacific
Musical

1. **Develop a vision or dream of what you want to achieve in your career**. This vision should include the type of work you would like to do and the positions you would like to hold. *There is nothing more powerful to the obtainment of career success than "locking on" to a specific vision of what you want to accomplish in a definite time period.* All the very successful people I've known have this "laser-like focus." They seem to thrive on the challenges involved, and more importantly, they never submit to failure. They just don't quit! They may fail from time to time, but they accept this as a part of the

If you do not think about the future and prepare for it, you will not have one.

Effective leaders are not satisfied with themselves. They have the courage to discover their shortcomings.

normal process of succeeding in the long term. They always keep trying until something good happens.

In formulating your career vision it is important that you be realistic in terms of how quickly you can achieve your goals. My generation grew up with the expectation that if you were an outstanding performer you would obtain a promotion every two or three years. This was possible because the economy was constantly expanding and there was little competition from abroad.

The business world is quite different today with sophisticated computer technology and free trade. From economic necessity, companies learned that they could do without several layers of middle management to compile and analyze data. In addition, the spread of quality programs has pushed down the responsibility for defect-free work from management to hourly personnel. The point is that today there are fewer promotional opportunities available. Therefore, it will take longer to climb the corporate ladder than in the past. A four- to six-year tenure in a management position is now becoming the norm for good performers in most companies. This "new reality" of the business world makes it even more important than ever that you augment your learning with other developmental activities. (See the end of this chapter for a summary of the key trends for the future that should be considered in developing your career vision.)

One final thought about developing a vision of what you want to achieve in your career: There is something magnetic about people who obviously enjoy their work and know where they are going in life. Good feelings and positive energy radiate from such people. In short, they become more promotable.

2. **Identify the leadership skills and knowledge necessary to achieve your vision.** This can best be determined by observing the skill sets of successful people in your field of interest. Also, from your reading, watch for trends that provide clues about the leadership skills that will be required in the future.

3. **Analyze your strengths and weaknesses** relative to the positions that you would like to hold. For example, if your goal is to someday become a product or division general manager, it would be advantageous to gain both sales and operations leadership experience early in your career. You may also want to polish your verbal presentation skills since they become increasingly important as you move up the management ladder.

   Insights on your strengths and weaknesses can be gained by completing the "Self-Appraisal of Leadership Effectiveness" in the following chapter.

4. **Seek leadership experiences and activities that help you overcome your weaknesses.** As a young person in your twenties and early thirties, you should try to obtain experience in many leadership situations both on and off the job. The idea is to gain as much practical leadership savvy as possible in the shortest amount of time.

   Some of this leadership experience should be abroad. With global trade now commonplace, business leaders must have a "worldview" about other cultures and markets. In many companies, foreign experience is a prerequisite for promotions into upper management.

   It is a good idea to establish a career path in a key functional area by the time you're thirty-five. The traditional key functional areas are marketing, sales, operations, finance, and human resources. If at all possible, try to stay away from specialty areas

In the business world, everyone is paid in two coins: cash and experience. Take the experience first; the cash will come later.

Harold Geneen, former CEO of AT&T

in your company that are not considered avenues to top jobs.

Do not bite off more than you can chew. The acquisition of leadership skills takes time and does not occur overnight. If you try to do too much too fast, you may get discouraged. Chances are you will abandon your program before it does any good.

None of the secrets of success will work unless you do.

5. **Stick with your program.** It takes desire and extra effort to improve yourself. You must continually work at it. Never be satisfied that you know enough to get by.

Preparing for more leadership responsibility in advance does not mean that you should neglect your present duties in any way. Rather, it means you should continue giving 100 percent and more. On the other hand, participate as well in one or two **outside** developmental activities on a regular basis. Here are a few suggestions:

1. **Get smart about computer technology**. You will not be able to effectively lead a large organization without a thorough knowledge of how to use the right mix of computer systems to make your operation more cost effective and more responsive to customers. Therefore, take a strong interest in keeping up-to-date about new computer technology and applications in your field. Read everything you can about the subject and seek the advice and input of technical experts.

Knowledge is power!

2. **Attend courses or seminars** that stress interpersonal relations and communication skills. These are the building blocks of leadership. An alternative would be to enroll in online courses that are offered by many universities. When you attend courses or seminars, always take notes. This doubles or triples your retention rate compared to just listening. It's surprising how few people take notes. What an opportunity missed!

3. **Assume a leadership role in a community organization.** This experience can provide valuable insights into how people function in groups and how they can be motivated.

4. **Read widely and extensively.** Your reading time should be split approximately in three ways: a) industry material to keep you up-to-date in your field, b) general business journals and newspapers to secure ideas and spot new business trends, and c) biographies and novels to provide leadership insights and stimulate creative thinking.

Today a reader, tomorrow a leader.
W. Fusselman

   People serious about their growth and development should spend at least two hours a day reading in the areas mentioned above. I find it convenient to read in the evenings or at lunch if I'm alone. Other people do it early in the morning. The reading schedule is not so important as the fact that it is done regularly. You will benefit immensely from such a practice in terms of enhancing your performance and being an interesting person to associate with.

5. **Become active in a leadership role with a professional or trade association.** This provides opportunities to practice leadership skills in a less threatening situation where your manager is not evaluating you. It also provides opportunities to develop relationships and friendships with successful people. A lot can be learned by associating with winners.

6. **Start a support group of trusted friends that are willing to discuss similar work related issues.** Hold weekly or monthly luncheons. This will provide valuable insights and ideas on leadership.

At this point you are probably thinking: "How can I find the time from my busy day to pursue outside developmental activities?" The answer lies in reallocating some of your unproductive time to productive time. Here are a few suggestions:

- Get up an hour earlier each morning.
- Reduce television time.
- Replace some sports time with study time and reflection.
- Read at lunch.
- Listen to developmental tapes in your car while commuting to and from work or appointments. The best-selling management and technical books are now available on audiotape. They can be obtained at bookstores, public libraries, and by ordering through the Internet.

The bottom line is most people can find at least ten hours a week of unproductive time that can be converted to productive developmental time. All it takes is the **desire** to do so.

People who acquire productive habits are far more likely to be successful than those who acquire unproductive habits.
Steven Covey
The Seven Habits of Highly Productive People

In addition to off-the-job activities, you can prepare yourself at work for greater leadership responsibility. One of the best ways to learn **on the job** is to seek out role models—leaders who are consistently producing outstanding results. Observe the role models in action to determine how they articulate a vision of the future and how they inspire others to achieve it. Watch how they handle pressure and how they lead by example. Note the values and principles upon which they make decisions. And most important of all, adopt the role models approaches with which you are most comfortable.

Cultivate in yourself the qualities you admire most in others.
Arnold Glason

You can also learn by watching weak leaders in action. Note how people react to their leadership styles. Ask yourself if you would have used the same approach, and if not, what would you have done?

Some managers have found it helpful to keep a daily journal of their observations of leaders in action. Such a habit stimulates innovative thinking about leadership. The journal also serves as an excellent reference source for future use.

Another way to develop leadership skills at work is to participate on cross-functional teams that are established to find solutions to performance problems that involve various divisions or departments in your company. These teams could be formed on a corporate, regional, or local level. Participating on them will broaden your horizons and expose you to the leadership styles of other executives. Whenever possible seek a leadership role on the teams. This will facilitate your selection as a presenter of the teams' recommendations to top management. Such exposure could be most helpful to your career. The best way to get involved on cross-functional teams is to let your manager know that you are interested.

Be careful, however, not to become so involved in cross-functional teams that your normal duties slip. Promotions are usually awarded to those who consistently add value to their organizations from performing in regular jobs. **Remember that your track record is what is most important.**

Promotion within your specialty area usually provides the best way to learn at a rapid pace, especially if it involves turning around a poorly performing division or department. Each turnaround situation requires unique strategies and tactics that must be devised and successfully implemented. This provides invaluable leadership experience.

Another approach for accelerating your on-the-job development is to seek lateral moves to different functional areas. As previously mentioned, you should seek such assignments early in your career and thereafter specialize in one or two key functional areas. You should make lateral moves only if they provide opportunities to acquire important new knowledge and skills.

Upward mobility in a company is primarily determined by acquiring and maintaining high visibility and exposure.
Eugene Jennings
Routes to the Executive Suite

Don't shy away from tough challenges— they offer the best opportunity to rapidly develop yourself.

Finally, taking a position in a different company can accelerate your development far beyond what could have occurred in your old company. In a new company you will suddenly be exposed to a new culture, different styles of leadership, and unique systems and processes—all of which will challenge you to quickly adapt and grow.

Before committing to a new employer, make sure that your values (the principles and standards that are important to you) match those of your new boss. A serious mismatch could quickly put you into an intolerable situation that could seriously damage your career.

The advantages of a self-development program are threefold. First, and most important, to grow and develop is stimulating and exciting. **The thrill of living is stretching out beyond what one thinks possible— constantly improving—becoming someone you are not yet today.** The realization that you are growing and developing is a powerful personal motivator, giving you a different outlook on life—an uplifting of spirits that enables you to better cope with the unpleasant aspects of work and personal problems. The daily nuisances of life do not appear so great when you are dealing on the higher plane of self-development. Second, the leadership skills and knowledge acquired from your self-development efforts will improve your qualifications for promotion. Third, when that promotion does come, you will be in a much better position to succeed than if you did nothing until the opportunity came your way. You will already have developed many of the leadership skills necessary for success in the new job.

It is easy to get into the comfortable rut of continually doing your job in the same old manner but then suddenly realizing that you are being passed up for promotions. The best way to keep this from happening is to perform in an outstanding manner and become

Try to work for an organization of people you admire.
Warren Buffett
Chairman, Berkshire Hathaway Inc.

Have the daring to accept yourself as a bundle of possibilities and undertake the game of making the most of your best.
Henry Emerson Fosdick

committed to a **continuous** program of self-improvement, both on and off the job. It is not so much how intense your developmental efforts are at one time, but the fact that you regularly work at it over extended periods.

If the idea of lifetime learning appears a bit overwhelming at this point in your career, remember the answer to the question: How does one go about eating an elephant? **One bite at a time!** The acquisition of vintage leadership skill is much like Vince Lombardi's definition of football: "a game of inches." The Chinese have another way of saying the same thing: "A journey of a thousand miles begins with a single step." **So approach the future with a vision in your mind of what you want to be, think of it often, and steadily, ever so steadily, work to make it happen by taking one small developmental step at a time. You will succeed if you approach your career in this fashion.**

Great things are not done by impulse but by a series of small things brought together.

Vincent Van Gogh

Key Trends for the Future That Should Be Considered in Developing Your Career Vision

- *Responsibility for decision-making will continue to be pushed to the lowest organizational levels. No matter what level you're at in an organization, you are responsible for results. You can't hide behind the old excuse that: "I didn't have the authority to make it happen."*

- *You can expect nothing but constant change in your company, so you must decide to welcome it and help shape it rather than fight it.*

- *Time-based competition will force companies to speed everything up faster and faster. The successful leaders will be those who can inspire their organizations to quickly respond to all types of issues with innovative approaches.*

- *There is only one marketplace: the world. You need to understand the key aspects of it.*

Key Requirements for Peak Leadership Performance

I.   *KEEP BALANCE IN YOUR LIFE*

II. *SEEK WORK THAT YOU ENJOY*

III. *KEEP IN SHAPE PHYSICALLY AND EMO-TIONALLY*

IV. *CONSTANTLY DEVELOP YOURSELF — ESPECIALLY IN LEADERSHIP SKILLS AND KNOWLEDGE OF NEW TECHNOLOGIES AND FOREIGN CULTURES*

IX

Appraising Your Leadership Effectiveness and Planning for Improvement

Art Bass, the former President of Federal Express and Chairman of Midway Airlines once told me, "Everyone is like a round dowel with a flat side." In other words, everyone has weaknesses. **The beautiful thing about life is that with all our flaws and flat sides, we can still aspire to any height if we are willing to invest the time and energy to do so.**

To improve your leadership performance, you first need to learn more about yourself—your strengths and weaknesses. Eric Hoffer said it best: "To become different from what we are, we must have some awareness of what we are."

You can obtain a comprehensive picture of your leadership capability by **honestly** answering the questions on the following pages. To obtain the maximum benefit from the exercise, I recommend that you complete a few pages each day for about a week. Reflect on each question before marking an answer. You will then be ready to proceed with the developmental steps presented at the end of this chapter.

For your convenience, the "Leadership Self Appraisal" is divided into three separate sections:

1. Internally Focused,
2. Team Focused, and
3. Maintaining Motivation and Momentum.

EFFECTIVE LEADERSHIP

INTERNALLY FOCUSED:

	ALWAYS	USUALLY	SOMETIMES	RARELY	Ideas or Actions To Improve (Notes)
1. Do you lead more from your interpersonal skills than from position or power?					
2. Do you set challenging but realistic performance standards?					
3. Do you expect and insist on excellence from yourself?					
4. Do you present a bearing that is confident?					
5. Do you keep your word?					
6. Do you have courage to handle defeat gracefully?					
7. Do you face conflict assertively?					
8. Do you maintain a sense of humor?					

INTERNALLY FOCUSED CONT:

	ALWAYS	USUALLY	SOMETIMES	RARELY	Ideas or Actions To Improve (Notes)
9. Do you keep confidences entrusted to you?					
10. Do you try to live by key company philosophies?					
11. Do you strive to develop an organizational climate that encourages open and free exchange of information?					
12. Do you assume responsibility for the actions of your team?					
13. Do you take time to enjoy the small but pleasant things in life?					
14. Do you keep in shape physically?					
15. Do you regularly save for the future?					
16. Do you remain calm during crises?					

EFFECTIVE LEADERSHIP

INTERNALLY FOCUSED:

	ALWAYS	USUALLY	SOMETIMES	RARELY	Ideas or Actions To Improve (Notes)
17. Do you control your temper?					
18. Do you keep your mind open to new ideas?					
19. Do you accept constructive criticism gracefully?					
20. Do you assume the blame when you make a mistake?					
21. Do you demonstrate total commitment to doing the best job possible?					
22. Do you introduce new company policies as your own instead of something imposed on you?					
23. Do you maintain good health habits?					
24. Do you willingly accept change?					

INTERNALLY FOCUSED CONT:

	ALWAYS	USUALLY	SOMETIMES	RARELY	*Ideas or Actions To Improve (Notes)*
25. Do you admit it when you do not have an answer?					
26. Do you maintain a cheerful, pleasant attitude?					
27. Do you spend personal time developing yourself for the future?					
28. Do you read books, take classes, and listen to tapes to continually learn?					

EFFECTIVE LEADERSHIP

TEAM-FOCUSED:

	ALWAYS	USUALLY	SOMETIMES	RARELY	Ideas or Actions To Improve (Notes)
30. Do you put the needs of your team above your own?					
31. Do you communicate a vision of the future to your co-workers?					
32. Do you regularly involve your team members in planning for the future?					
33. Do you encourage and inspire everyone to give his or her best?					
34. Do you assist employees in satisfying their work related needs?					
35. Do you "go to bat" for your people with upper management?					
36. Do you hold people accountable for their actions?					
37. Do you treat everyone in a Fair but firm manner?					

TEAM-FOCUSED CONT.

	ALWAYS	USUALLY	SOMETIMES	RARELY	Ideas or Actions To Improve (Notes)
38. Do you give credit to those who make suggestions?					
39. Do you trust your people until proven otherwise?					
40. Do you bring out the best in people by showing confidence in them?					
41. Do you provide abundant performance feedback to all your people?					
42. Do you openly show appreciation for their efforts?					
43. Do you give people the freedom to express opinions that might differ from yours?					
44. Do you recognize the achievements of your team members?					
45. Do you share information openly and willingly?					

EFFECTIVE LEADERSHIP

TEAM-FOCUSED CONT.

	ALWAYS	USUALLY	SOMETIMES	RARELY	Ideas or Actions To Improve (Notes)
46. Do you give high priority to resolving team members problems and compaints?					
47. Do you let team members know what is expected of them?					
48. Do you encourage ideas and suggestions?					
49. Do you put directives in the form of a request, rather than a demand?					
50. Do you involve your team members in decision making?					
51. Do you encourage people to think on their own?					
52. Do you explain the reasons for why you accept or reject suggestions and ideas?					

TEAM-FOCUSED CONT.

	ALWAYS	USUALLY	SOMETIMES	RARELY	Ideas or Actions To Improve (Notes)
53. Do you let people perform in their own style?					
54. Do you delegate as much as possible?					
55. Do you ensure that the workplace is clean, safe, and comfortable?					
56. Do you maintain an open mind when someone questions something about your operation?					
57. Do you point out to team members areas that need improvement?					
58. Do you treat everyone with respect, dignity, and courtesy?					
59. Do you go out of your way to work as a team member?					

EFFECTIVE LEADERSHIP

TEAM-FOCUSED CONT.

	ALWAYS	USUALLY	SOMETIMES	RARELY	Ideas or Actions To Improve (Notes)
60. Do you encourage people to assume greater responsibility for doing their jobs better?					
61. Do you evenly enforce policies and regulations?					
62. Do you give individuals opportunities to develop their own ideas?					
63. Do you actively coach your team and its members?					
64. Do you strive to remember the names of all the people you work with?					
65. Do you take disciplinary action when warranted?					
66. Do you maintain a positive attitude toward everything done in your department?					

MAINTAINING MOTIVATION AND MOMENTUM:

	ALWAYS	USUALLY	SOMETIMES	RARELY	Ideas or Actions To Improve (Notes)
67. Do you visualize what is necessary for the long-term success of your organization?					
68. Do you continually seek new and better ways to reach your organization's goals?					
69. Do you act on performance violations immediately?					
70. Do you take time to explain the reasons for changes?					
71. Do you listen carefully?					
72. Do you try to instill in your team the desire to be the best — number one?					
73. Do you actively seek promotional opportunities for your outstanding performers?					

EFFECTIVE LEADERSHIP

MAINTAINING MOTIVATION AND MOMENTUM:

	ALWAYS	USUALLY	SOMETIMES	RARELY	Ideas or Actions To Improve (Notes)
74. Do you regularly spend time with your people?					
75. Do you try to anticipate what could go wrong in your operation?					
76. Do you take action in advance to prevent possible problems?					
77. Do you make difficult decisions without procrastination?					
78. Do you concentrate on the areas of the job that have the highest payoff?					
79. Do you set daily and weekly priorities of what you want to accomplish?					
80. Do you maintain a sense of urgency for meeting team targets?					
81. Do you work hard at removing the obstacles that hinder the performance of your team?					

After answering all the questions, go back over your responses to identify those marked "always" and "rarely." Your leadership strengths are identified by your "always" answers. This knowledge is important because **successful leaders build on their strengths.** They seek positions where they know they can shine.

This important strategy can be limiting if you have serious weaknesses that are not corrected or minimized—for example the inability to get along with colleagues or to plan ahead for the future. The people who continually advance in their companies are those that leverage their strengths and never stop trying to overcome their deficiencies.

You cannot run away from a weakness. You must sometimes fight it out or perish; and if that be so, why not now, and where you stand?

Robert Louis Stevenson

With this in mind, review the questions answered "rarely." These areas require work. Use the space on the right-hand side of each page to jot down ideas on how to improve. For example, if you infrequently involve your personnel in planning for the future, you may decide to improve by holding quarterly planning meetings.

After thinking about all the questions marked "rarely," rank them according to the priority of importance to your career. Then, employing the philosophy of taking one step or bite at a time, develop and implement your improvement program. As you do so, carefully monitor the results and reactions of direct reports and peers. Obtain their feedback. If the early results are positive, continue in the direction that you are headed. Negative feedback should be evaluated to determine where you went wrong.

As you work toward improving your leadership skills, do not expect success overnight. Be patient with yourself; it takes time to transform a new way of behaving into a comfortable habit. Your people also need time to adjust to changes in your style. At first, they may be suspicious. As you demonstrate consistency over time, they will respond favorably with such comments as, "The boss has sure changed for the better."

The only thrill worthwhile is the one that comes from making something out of yourself.

William Feather

The fruits of your self-development labors will be many. Besides opening up salary advancement and promotional opportunities, you will gain a sense of accomplishment by becoming a more competent leader. Your esteem in the organization will grow. **Above all, you will have improved your capacity to participate in one of life's richest experiences—helping others reach their highest potential.** The lives of your personnel and colleagues will be better for having known you.

X

Other Inspiring Quotations on Leadership Attributes and Ideals Worth Emulating

One of the great joys of life is discovering new insights into human nature in general and yourself in particular. From the observations of poets, statesmen, writers, and business executives comes a wealth of wisdom that provides understanding, guidance, and inspiration for leaders or potential leaders in all walks of life.

In this section you will learn from the likes of Churchill, Emerson, Schweitzer, Jefferson, Iacocca, Walton, Peale, Edison, Lincoln, Twain, King, and many others. You will find that their words speak to you or have relevance for you in different ways as conditions and situations change in your life. At one time, a saying may lead you to discover an important truth about yourself, strengthen a conviction, or reinforce an important value. At another time, the words may inspire you to take action in an area where you had not previously planned to do so. **But most of all, the thoughts expressed will help you take the "high road" in your dealings with others. In effect, they become your "guideposts" for living your life by the highest standards and ideals.**

Hence, refer often to the treasury of quotations found on the following pages and throughout the book. Memorize those that are most meaningful to you. Most of all, enjoy the feelings expressed. As William Ellery Channing tells us: "Quotations are true levelers. They give, to all who will faithfully use them, the spiritual presence of the best and greatest of the human race."

Aim at the sun, and you may not reach it; but your arrow will fly far higher than if you aimed at an object on a level with yourself.
J. Howse

Finish each day and be done with it . . . you have done what you could; some blunders and absurdities no doubt crept in; forget them as soon as you can. Tomorrow is a new day; you shall begin it well and serenely.
Ralph Waldo Emerson

The gem cannot be polished without friction, nor man perfected without trials.
Chinese Proverb

One man can completely change the character of a country, and the industry of its people, by dropping a single seed in fertile soil.
John C. Gifford

I don't know what your destiny will be, but one thing I know: the only ones among you who will be really happy are those who will have sought and found how to serve.

Dr. Albert Schweitzer

If you think you can, or you think you can't, you're probably right.

Mark Twain

Any man who is honest, fair, tolerant, kindly, charitable of others, and well behaved is a success, no matter what his station in life.

Jay E. House

Faith without works is like a bird without wings; though she may hop about on earth, she will never fly to heaven. But when both are joined together, then can the soul mount up to her eternal nest.

Beaumont

A leader is best when people barely know he exists . . . when his work is done, his aim fulfilled, they will say, we did this ourselves.

Lao-Tse

Three men were laying brick.
The first was asked, "What are you doing?"
He answered, "Laying some brick."
The second man was asked, "What are you working for?"
He answered, "Five dollars a day."
The third man was asked, "What are you doing?"
He answered, "I am helping to build a great Cathedral."
Which man are you?
> *Charles Schwab*

Character is the foundation stone upon which one must build to win respect. Just as no worthy building can be erected on a weak foundation, so no lasting reputation worthy of respect can be built on a weak character. Without character, all effort to attain dignity is superficial, and results are sure to be disappointing.
> *R. C. Samsel*

Real joy comes not from ease or riches or from the praise of men, but from doing something worthwhile.
> *Sir Wilfred Grenfell*

No matter how good or how smart you are, sooner or later that wave will come and knock down what you have worked so hard to build up. And when that happens, only the person who has somebody's hand to hold will be able to laugh.
> *Rabbi Harold S. Kushner*

The law of harvest is to reap more than you sow. Sow an act, and you reap a habit; sow a habit, and you reap a character; sow a character, and you reap a destiny.
G. D. Boardman

The man who lives for himself is a failure; the man who lives for others has achieved true success.
Norman Vincent Peale

Happiness is a by-product of an effort to make someone else happy.
Greta Palmer

Every worthwhile accomplishment, big or little, has its stages of drudgery and triumph; a beginning, a struggle, and a victory.
Anonymous

I know the price of success—dedication, hard work, and unremitting devotion to the things you want to see happen.
Frank Lloyd Wright

Nearly all men can stand adversity, but if you want to test a man's character, give him power.
Abraham Lincoln

Difficulties mastered are opportunities won.
Winston Churchill

The world stands aside to let anyone pass who knows where he is going.
David Starr Gordon

He who is false to the present duty breaks a thread in the loom, and you will see the effect when the weaving of a lifetime is unraveled.
William Ellery Channing

If you can give your children only one gift, let it be enthusiasm.
Bruce Barton

Plant the seeds of expectation in your mind; cultivate thoughts that anticipate achievement. Believe in yourself as being capable of overcoming all obstacles and weaknesses.
    Norman Vincent Peale

Whether our efforts are, or are not, favored by life, let us be able to say, when we come near the great goal, I have done what I could.
    Louis Pasteur

If there be any truer measure of a man than what he does, it must be what he gives.
    Robert South

Read every day something no one else is reading. Think every day something no one else is thinking. It is bad for the mind to be always a part of unanimity.
    Christopher Morley

Those who have not sown anything during their responsible life will have nothing to reap in the future.
    George Gurdjieff

I believe the first test of a truly great man is humility.
John Ruskin

It is better to create than to be learned; creating is the true
essence of life.
Niebuhr

Nothing is impossible to a willing heart.
John Heywood

By constant self-discipline and self-control you can
develop greatness of character.
Grenville Kleiser

The man who has accomplished all that he thinks
worthwhile has begun to die.
E. T. Trigg

Progress results from persistence with purpose.
    Frank Tyger

There is one element that is worth its weight in gold, and that is loyalty. It will cover a multitude of weaknesses.
    Philip Armour

We grow great by dreams.
    Woodrow Wilson

Life can only be understood backward, but it must be lived forward.
    Niels Bohr

Failure should challenge us to new heights of accomplishment, not pull us to new depths of despair. Failure is delay, not defeat. It is a temporary detour, not a dead-end street.
    William Arthur Ward

It is not the strength, but the duration of great sentiments that makes great men.
Friedrich Nietzsche

Ideas go booming through the world louder than cannons. Thoughts are mightier than armies. Principles have achieved more victories than horsemen or chariots.
W. M. Paxton

Strong convictions precede great actions.
Author Unknown

Great necessity elevates man; petty necessity casts him down.
Goethe

Back of every noble life there are principles that have fashioned it.
George H. Lorimer

You are already of consequence in the world if you are known as a man of strict integrity.
Grenville Kleiser

Any man worth his salt will stick up for what he believes right, but it takes a slightly bigger man to acknowledge instantly and without reservation that he is in error.
Gen. Peyton C. March

Half of the world is on the wrong scent in the pursuit of happiness. They think it consists in having and getting, and in being served by others. It consists in giving and serving others.
Henry Drummond

Live your life each day as you would climb a mountain. An occasional glance toward the summit keeps the goal in mind, but many beautiful scenes are to be observed from each new vantage point. Climb slowly, steadily, enjoying each passing moment, and the view from the summit will serve as a fitting climax for the journey.
Harold V. Melchert

Who dares nothing, need hope for nothing.
Johann Schiller

In matters of principle, stand like a rock.

Thomas Jefferson

No success is worth giving up on your integrity.

Dennis Waitley

He who cherishes a beautiful vision, a lofty ideal in his heart, will one day realize it.

James Allen

It is not who is right but what is right that is of importance.

Thomas Huxley

Ideas control the world.

James A. Garfield

The real difference between men is energy. A strong will, a settled purpose, an invincible determination can accomplish almost anything, and in this lies the distinction between great men and little men.
Thomas Fuller

Pride is at the bottom of all great mistakes.
John Ruskin

A reputation for a thousand years may depend upon the conduct of a single moment.
Ernest Bramah

When people are made to feel secure and important and appreciated, it will no longer be necessary for them to whittle down others in order to seem bigger in comparison.
Virginia Arcastle

Commit to your business. I think I overcame every single one of my shortcomings by the sheer passion I brought to my work.
> *Sam Walton*

Compassion is the basis of all morality.
> *Arthur Schopenhauer*

If you play it safe in life, you've decided that you don't want to grow anymore.
> *Shirley Hufstedler*

We're worn into grooves by time—by our habits. In the end, these grooves are going to show whether we've been second rate or champions.
> *Frank B. Gilbert*

What a man does for others, not what they do for him, gives him immortality.
> *Daniel Webster*

There is nothing in the world so much admired as a man who knows how to bear unhappiness with courage.
>   *Seneca*

Half of the harm that is done in this world is due to people who want to feel important . . . they do not mean to do harm . . . they are absorbed in the endless struggle to think well of themselves.
>   *T. S. Eliot*

Success is not due to a fortuitous concourse of stars at our birth, but to a steady trial of sparks from the grindstone of hard work each day.
>   *Kenneth Hildebrand*

Take the course opposite to custom and you will almost always do well.
>   *Jean Jacques Rousseau*

There is no elevator to success—you have to take one step at a time.
>   *Author Unknown*

As a man grows older . . .
　　. . . he values the voice of experience more and the
　　voice of prophecy less.
　　. . . he finds more of life's wealth in the common
　　pleasures—home, health, and children.
　　. . . he thinks more about the work of men and less
　　about their wealth.
　　. . . he begins to appreciate his own father a little more.
　　. . . he hurries less, and usually makes more progress.
　　. . . he esteems the friendship of God a little higher.
　　　　Roy L. Smith

The four-way test of the things we think, say, or do:
　　. . . Is it the truth?
　　. . . Is it fair to all concerned?
　　. . . Will it build good will and better friendships?
　　. . . Will it be beneficial to all concerned?
　　　　Rotary International Motto

He who wishes to fulfill his mission in the world must be a
man of one idea, that is, of one great overmastering
purpose, overshadowing all his aims, and guiding and
controlling his entire life.
　　　　Bate

When a man realizes his littleness, his greatness can
appear.
　　　　H. G. Wells

The rung of a ladder was never meant to rest upon, but only to hold a man's foot long enough to enable him to put the other somewhat higher.
Thomas Huxley

If a man lives a decent life and does his work fairly and squarely so that those dependent upon him and attached to him are better for his having lived, then he is a success.
Teddy Roosevelt

The bird of paradise alights only upon the hand that does not grasp.
John Berry

Do not waste a minute—not a second—in trying to demonstrate to others the merits of your performance. If your work does not indicate itself, you cannot vindicate it.
Thomas W. Higginson

Prosperity is a great teacher; adversity, a greater.
William Haylitt

Any man can work when every stroke of his hand brings down the fruit rattling from the tree to the ground; but to labor in season and out of season, under every discouragement, by the power of truth—that requires a heroism which is transcendent.
Henry Ward Beecher

A really great man is known by three signs—generosity in the design, humanity in the execution, moderation in success.
Bismark

You can buy a man's time, you can even buy his physical presence at a given place, but you cannot buy enthusiasm . . . you cannot buy loyalty . . . you cannot buy the devotion of hearts, minds, or souls. You must earn these.
Charles Frances

Every man has a right to his opinions, but no man has a right to be wrong in his facts.
Bernard M. Baruch

Success is where preparation and opportunity meet.
        Bobby Unser

We become winners by overcoming life's hurdles.
        Dr. Norman Vincent Peale

There is no fire like passion; there is no shark like hatred;
there is no snare like folly; there is no torrent like greed.
        Buddha

It is only when you are pursued that you become swift.
        Kahil Gibran

A father can do nothing better for his children than to
love their mother.
        Author Unknown

Begin not with a program, but with a deed.
        Florence Nightingale

The speed of the boss is the speed of the team.
  Lee Iacocca

Thank God—every morning when you get up—that you have something to do which must be done, whether you like it or not. Being forced to work, and forced to do your best, will breed in you a hundred virtues that the idle never know.
  Charles Kingsley

It's no exaggeration to say that a strong positive self-image is the best possible preparation for success in life.
  Dr. Joyce Brothers

As the essence of courage is to stake one's life on a possibility, so the essence of faith is to believe that the possibility exists.
  William Salter

From those to whom much is given, much is required.
  John F. Kennedy

Love is the most important ingredient for success. Without it, your life echoes emptiness. With it, your life vibrates warmth and meaning.
The Best of Success

There is no road too long to the man who advances deliberately and without undue haste; no honors too distant to the man who prepares himself for them with patience.
Bruyers

I've felt that dissatisfaction is the basis of progress. When we become satisfied in business, we become obsolete.
J. W. "Bill" Marriott, Sr.

Show me a man that you honor, and I will know what kind of man you are, for it shows me what your ideal of manhood is, and what kind of a man you long to be.
Thomas Carlyle

Life is a two-stage rocket. The first is physical energy—it ignites, and we are off. As physical energy diminishes, the spiritual stage must ignite to boost us into orbit, or we will fall back or plateau.
F. Smith (Dallas, Texas)

Plant the seeds of expectation in your mind; cultivate thoughts that anticipate achievement. Believe in yourself as being capable of overcoming all obstacles and weaknesses.
Norman Vincent Peale

To do something, however small, to make others happier and better is the highest ambition, the most elevating hope, which can inspire a human being.
John Lubbock

Many of the greatest men have owed their success to industry rather than cleverness.
John Lubbock

The time is always right to do what is right.
    Martin Luther King, Jr.

There's no gain without pain.
    Benjamin Franklin

If you will call your troubles experiences, and remember that every experience develops some latent force within you, you will grow vigorous and happy, however adverse your circumstances may seem to be.
    John R. Miller

Riches without charity are worth nothing. They are a blessing only to him who makes them a blessing to others.
    Henry Fielding

To keep the lamp burning, we have to keep putting oil in it.
    Mother Teresa

Be careful of your thoughts, for your thoughts become
words.

Be careful of your words, for your words become actions.

Be careful of your actions, for your actions become
habits.

Be careful of your habits, for your habits become your
character.

Be careful of your character, for your character becomes
your destiny.

Author Unknown

RESOLUTION

Whereas the Supreme Power of the universe has deemed it natural to create human beings of various colors, races, and creeds; and

Whereas in his sight they all are his equally beloved children;

Therefore be it resolved that there is no superior race or group of peoples and that all men are brothers of equal rank; and be it further resolved that we know this and believe it now and forever!

W. Newman

XI

Encouragement for Leaders or Aspiring Leaders

With so much involved in effectively leading others, **is it all really possible?** It is my unshakable belief, born from years of leading and studying leaders, that any person endowed with normal intelligence and who likes people can rise to the highest levels of an organization. Sadly, most people tap into only 8 or 10 percent of their total potential. Even those who are considered great leaders utilize only 15 to 20 percent of their capabilities.

Your level of achievement, therefore, depends on one key factor—your willingness and desire. As Thomas Edison said, "If we were to do all the things we're capable of doing, we would literally astonish ourselves."

With all the qualities I have subscribed to effective leaders, one might think that they are not human. Abraham Zalenik puts it all in perspective in the first paragraph of his book *Human Dilemmas of Leadership:*

> *The most self-conscious people in the world are its leaders. They may also be the most anxious and insecure. As men of action, leaders face risks and uncertainty, and often display remarkable courage in shouldering grave responsibility. But beneath their fortitude, there often lies an agonizing sense of doubt and a need to justify themselves.*

From the little spark may burst a mighty flame.
Dante

One final question needs to be addressed: Is the profession of leadership, with all its inherent problems, toil and tribulation, worth the effort? The answer, of course, depends on your perspective. If you take the broad view, in terms of what the leader can do to make people feel good about themselves and help them succeed, there is no question about the value of the profession. A leader in management has the opportunity to favorably influence his or her personnel for more than half of their waking hours. **What an opportunity to serve others and help shape the future of mankind.**

XII

The Secrets of Effective Leadership

The Secrets of Effective Leadership

I.   TREAT EVERYONE WITH RESPECT AND DIGNITY.

II.   SET THE EXAMPLE FOR OTHERS TO FOLLOW.

III.   BE AN ACTIVE COACH.

IV.   MAINTAIN THE HIGHEST STANDARDS OF HONESTY
        AND INTEGRITY

V.   INSIST ON EXCELLENCE AND HOLD YOUR PEOPLE
        ACCOUNTABLE.

VI.   BUILD GROUP COHESIVENESS AND PRIDE.

VII.   SHOW CONFIDENCE IN YOUR PEOPLE.

VIII.   MAINTAIN A STRONG SENSE OF URGENCY.

IX.   BE AVAILABLE AND VISIBLE TO YOUR TEAM.

X.   DEVELOP YOURSELF TO YOUR HIGHEST POTENTIAL.

Secrets of Effective Leadership

This book can be used in a variety of ways to develop the leadership skills of your management team. Some suggestions:

- Distribute the book to managers and team leaders with a cover letter
- Hand it out at management conferences
- Use it in conjunction with management training programs

ALSO AVAILABLE

Spirit of Leadership:
WISDOM OF THE AGES

A unique collection of quotations on the art of leading others from the observations of famous statesmen, generals, poets, writers and business executives. 270 pages of wisdom to guide and inspire leaders.

Sample topics in *SPIRIT OF LEADERSHIP:*

- Leadership Ideals
- Excellence
- Courage
- Setting the Example
- Inspiring Employees
- Life's Lessons
- Possibilities
- Requirements for Success

An Ideal Book For:

- Personal Development
- Inspiration
- Speech Writing
- Thoughtful Gifts
- Leadership Courses

Quantity discounts are available for orders from 3 to 1000 books. For information write:

Director of Marketing
Leadership Education and Development, Inc.
113 First Avenue
Mount Pleasant, TN. 38474
Phone: 1-800-659-6135
www.leadershipdevelopment.com

Successful leaders make it look easy...
find out how they do it.

Inspired leadership is a key element of any successfully managed organization. The world's best leaders have learned how to draw upon critical resources, at the precise moment they are needed.

At **www.leadershipdevelopment.com** you can quickly access an online leadership guide — the latest and most comprehensive leadership information available. This guide is designed to provide immediate access to the resources you need, at the moment you need them.

Whatever the challenge — handling rapid growth, restructuring, cost cutting, conflict resolution, or negotiation — our online leadership guide provides the practical information you need to quickly prepare solutions that will succeed.

And to motivate and reward your staff, or share your vision with your team, our superbly crafted awards, plaques, and gifts can be used to communicate the values you want to reinforce in your organization.

So, whether you're preparing a seminar, setting up a training program, trying to stimulate change, or seeking guidance and inspiration, visit www.leadershipdevelopment.com and then lead the way!

www.leadershipdevelopment.com

XIII

References

PREFACE
1. T. J. Larkin and Sandar Larkin, "Reaching and Changing Frontline Employees, *Harvard Business Review,* May-June 1996.

I.   WHAT IS LEADERSHIP
1. Mary Parker Follett, *Dynamic Administration* (NewYork: Harper & Row Publishers, 1941), p. 143.
2. Robert Levering, Milton Moskowitz, and Michael Katz, *The 100 Best Companies to Work for in America* (New York: New American Library, 1985), p. 110.
3. Baldwin H. Ward, ed., *The Great Innovators* (New York: Year Inc., 1970), p. 157.
4. John Naisbitt and Patricia Aburdene, *Re-inventing the Corporation* (New York: Warner Books, Inc. 1985), p.24.
5. Harold Geneen, *Managing* (Garden City: Doubleday and Company, Inc., 1984), p. 146.

III. THE DEVELOPMENT OF LEADERSHIP STYLE
1. Dwight D. Eisenhower, *At Ease: Stories I Tell to Friends* (New York: Doubleday and Company, Inc., 1967), p. 136.
2. Ibid.

IV. PROFILE OF AN EFFECTIVE LEADER
1. Bruce Catton, *The Army of the Potomac: A Stillness at Appomattox* (Garden City: Doubleday and Company, Inc., 1953), p. 44.
2. Ibid.
3. Ibid.
4. Betsey Morris, "He's Smart. He's Not Nice. He's Saving Big Blue," *Fortune,* April 14, 1997.

References

1. THE EFFECTIVE LEADER BUILDS GROUP COHESIVE-
    NESS AND PRIDE
    1. Jack Brennan, "Patriots Grateful for Berry," *The
       Commercial Appeal,* January 14, 1986.
    2. Warren Bennis and Bert Nanus, *Leaders* (New York:
       Harper and Row Publishers, 1985), p. 30.
    3. Marilyn Much, "Campbell Soup's Johnson," *Investor's
       Business Daily,* March 26, 1997.
    4. Richard Rapport, "To Build a Winning Team: An
       Interview with Head Coach Bill Walsh," *Harvard
       Business Review,* January-February 1993.
    5. Ibid.

2. THE EFFECTIVE LEADER LIVES BY THE HIGHEST
    STANDARDS OF HONESTY AND INTEGRITY
    1. "Managers Rank Competence and Integrity as Most
       Desired Values," *Management Review,* September
       1982.
    2. *Bits and Pieces,* October 1985.
    3. Thomas F. Boyle, "More 'Honesty' Tests Used to Gauge
       Worker's Morale," *Wall Street Journal,* July 11, 1985.
    4. Morgan W. McCall, Jr., and Michael M. Lombardo,
       "What Makes a Top Executive?" *Psychology Today,*
       February, 1983.
    5. Robert S. Wieder, "Dr. Truth," *Success.*
    6. Ibid.
    7. Kenneth Blanchard and Norman Vincent Peale, *The
       Power of Ethical Management* (New York: Fawcett Crest
       1988), p. 20.
    8. The Rotary International Motto.
    9. Blanchard and Peale, *The Power of Ethical
       Management,* p. 20.

4. THE EFFECTIVE LEADER COACHES TO IMPROVE PERFORMANCE
   1. Hendrie D. Weisinger, "The Art of Better Constructive Criticism—Giving and Taking," *Boardroom Reports,* August 15, 1991.
   2. *Boardroom Reports,* April, 1985, (Interview with Mary Kay Ash).

5. THE EFFECTIVE LEADER INSISTS ON EXCELLENCE
   1. *Boardroom Reports,* October 15, 1986.
   2. "Bringing Out the Best in People," *Reader's Digest,* October, 1986. (Condensed from the book *Bringing Out the Best in People* by Alan Loy McGinnis) {Minneapolis: Augsburg Publishing House, 1985}, p. 98.
   3. Ibid.
   4. McGinnis, *Bringing Out the Best in People,* p. 98.

6. THE EFFECTIVE LEADER SETS THE EXAMPLE FOR OTHERS TO FOLLOW
   1. *Wall Street Journal,* May 30, 1984. (Advertisement by Shearson Lehman American Express.)
   2. "Tom Watson Looks at the Past and the Present," *Wall Street Journal,* April 7, 1986.
   3. *Bits and Pieces,* October 1985.
   4. John T. Molloy, *Molloy's Live for Success* (New York: Bantam Books, 1983), p. 2.
   5. Naisbitt and Aburdene, *Re-inventing the Corporation.* p. 85.
   6. Michael Korda, "Ten Steps to Success before 40", *Reader's Digest,* December 1989.
   7. Bennis and Nanus, *Leaders,* p. 70.
   8. Ibid.

References

8. THE EFFECTIVE LEADER HAS COURAGE
    1. Donald T. Phillips, *Lincoln on Leadership* (New York: Warner Books, 1992), p. 66.
    2. Jackie Robinson, *Baseball Has Done It* (Philadelphia: J B. Lippincott Company, 1941), p.51
    3. Sandy Grady, *USA Today*, April 3, 1997.

10. THE EFFECTIVE LEADER IS DECISIVE
    1. Matt Krantz, "UAL Corp's Gerald Greenwald: Preparing for Business Battle with Adventures in the Wild," *Investor's Business Daily*, August 27, 1997.

11. THE EFFECTIVE LEADER HAS A STRONG SENSE OF URGENCY
    1. Thomas J. Peters and Robert H. Waterman, Jr., *In Search of Excellence* (New York: Harper and Row, 1982), p. 119.
    2. Edward V. Rickenbacker, *Rickenbacker* (Englewood Cliffs: Prentice-Hall, Inc., 1967), p. 400.

12. THE EFFECTIVE LEADER MAKES EVERY MINUTE COUNT
    1. Andrew S. Grove, "Your Most Precious Resource: Your Time," *The Wall Street Journal of Management*, (Homewood: Dow Jones-Irwin Inc., 1985), p. 6.
    2. Allen Deutschman, "The CEO's Secret of Managing Time," *Fortune*, June 1, 1992.
    3. Ibid.

15. THE EFFECTIVE LEADER LISTENS TO SUBORDINATES
    1. James MacGregor Burns, *Leadership* (New York: Harper & Row, Publishers, 1978). P. 374

16. THE EFFECTIVE LEADER IS DETERMINED
   1. Hugh Sidney, "Above All, the Man Had Character," *Time,* February 21, 1983.
   2. Baldwin H. Ward, *The Great Innovators,* p. 90
   3. Daniel J. Murphy, "Aviator Billy Mitchell: How He Sacrificed His Career to Champion Air Force," *Investor's Business Daily,* December 3, 1997.
   4. Ibid.
   5. Geoffrey C. Ward, "How Teddy Roosevelt Took Charge," *Success.*
   6. Ibid.
   7. Jack Canfield and Mark Victor Hansen, *Chicken Soup for the Soul* (Deerfield Beach: Health Communications, Inc., 1993), p. 229.
   8. Peggy Reisser, "Churchill Casts a Long Shadow," *The Commercial Appeal,* September 17, 1985.

17. THE EFFECTIVE LEADER IS AVAILABLE AND VISIBLE TO HIS OR HER STAFF
   1. David Ogilvy, *"Leadership—The Forgotten Factor in Management,"* (A Charles Coolidge Parlin Memorial Lecture, May 10, 1972).
   2. John Holusha, "Grace Pastiak's Web of Inclusion," *New York Times,* May 5, 1991.
   3. *Wall Street Journal,* October 26, 1992.

VI HOW TO KEEP YOUR HEALTH BY MANAGING STRESS
   1. Sally Ann Stewart, "Burnout Woes? Join the Crowd," *USA Today,* December 23, 1985.
   2. Herbert Benson and Robert L. Allen, "How Much Stress Is Too Much?" *Harvard Review,* September-October 1980.
   3. *Bottom Line-Personal,* April 30, 1984.

References

4. Perry Pascarella, "What Makes a Good Manager," *Future Focus—Advancement and Leadership Strategies* (New York: Industry Week, 1984), p. 55.
5. Dr. Lee Salk, "The Other Side of Retirement Planning," *Bottom Line-Personal,* June 30, 1986.
6. Sue Shellenbarger, "No You're Not too Tough to Suffer a Bout of Burnout," *Wall Street Journal,* June 25, 1997.
7. Daniel Goleman, *Emotional Intelligence* (New York: Bantam Books, 1995.)
8. Ibid.
9. Ralph LaForge, "Exercise, Self-Esteem, and the Mini-Boost," *Executive Health,* January, 1987.
10. Pam Harrison, "So What's Stopping You?" *Today's Health,* February 15, 1986 and *USA Today,* February 7, 1986.
11. *Bottom Line-Personal,* February 15, 1986 and *USA Today,* February 7, 1986.
12. *Bottom Line-Personal,* March 15, 1984.
13. Benson and Allen, "How Much Stress Is Too Much?" p. 87.
14. *Bottom Line-Personal,* March 30, 1984.
15. Jonathan D. Brown, *Bottom Line-Personal,* April 30, 1987.
16. *Bottom Line-Personal,* September 30, 1985, (From study at Harvard University published in the *Journal of the American Medical Association).*
17. *Bottom Line-Personal,* January 20, 1984.
18. Mary Powers, "Breaking the Habit Called Best for Life," *The Commercial Appeal,* November 18, 1965.
19. Sally Ann Stewart, "Fish Oil Lowers Cholesterol", *USA Today,* November 13, 1985.
20. Mary Powers, "Breaking the Habit," p. A1.
21. *Business Week,* January 27, 1986.
22. *Bottom Line-Personal,* September 15, 1985. (From Stanford University study cited in *Men's Health.*)

23. *Bottom Line-Personal,* January 30, 1984.
24. John W. Travis and Regina Sara Ryan, "Wellness—Small Changes Can Make a Big Difference," *Bottom Line-Personal,* September 15, 1992.
25. *Executive Health,* (November 3, 1992).
26. Paul G. Engel, "Unwinding—How CEOs Escape The Pressures of Business," *Industry Week,* December 20, 1985.
27. Ibid.
28. *Bottom Line-Personal,* August 15, 1985.
29. *Bits and Pieces,* July 1982.
30. "Lessons in Happiness and Success from Sir John Templeton," *Bottom Line-Personal,* September 1, 1997.
31. Dennis Waitley, *Seeds of Greatness* (Old Tappan: Fleming H. Revell Co., 1983), p. 162.
32. Ibid.

VII. STRIVING FOR A MORE SATISFYING PERSONAL LIFE
1. *Bottom Line-Personal,* June 30, 1986.
2. Daniel Goleman, "Strategies For Shaking Gloom Are Emerging From New Studies", *New York Times,* December 30, 1992.
3. *Bottom Line-Personal,* August 30, 1985.
4. Leo F. Buscaglia, Ph.D., "On the Challenges of Relationships," *Executive Health,* December 1986.
5. *Bottom Line-Personal,* October 1986.
6. *Reader's Digest,* March 1986.
7. *Wall Street Journal,* January 11, 1993.
8. Dennis Waitley, *Seeds of Greatness.*

VIII. LEADERSHIP SELF-DEVELOPMENT—A LIFETIME PURSUIT
1. Bennis and Nanus, *Leaders,* p. 188.
2. Ibid.

References

3. Joseph Nocera, "Living with Layoffs," *Fortune,* April 1, 1996.
4. Stratford Sherman, "A Brave New Darwinian Workplace," *Fortune,* January 25, 1993.
5. Ibid.
6. Louis S. Richman, "How to Protect Your Financial Future," *Fortune,* January 23, 1993.
7. Interview with Bill Gates and Warren Buffett, *Fortune,* July 20, 1998.

XIV

Index

Index

Index

Index

V

Vacations, 169-170
Vail, Theodore N., 233
Van Gogh, Vincent, 189
Visibility, 124-128
Vision, 3-7, 29, 36, 99, 181-182, 190

W

Wade, Bill, 16, 58
Waitley, Dennis, 159, 222
Wall Street, 38, 84
Wall Street Journal, 165
Wallenda Factor, 73
Wallenda, Karl, 73
Wal-mart, 64
Walsh, Bill, 35
Walton, Sam, 45, 64, 211, 224
Wanamaker, John, 155
Ward, William Arthur, 219
Washington, Booker T., 86
Washington, General George, 82, 120
Washington Monument, 4
Waterloo, 124
Waterman, Robert, 90, 124
Watson, Jr., Thomas, 65
Webster, Daniel, 224
Welch, Jack, 40
Wellington, Duke of, 124
Wells, H.G., 226
West Point, 19, 108
Wilde, Oscar, 166
Willmott, Pete, 27-28, 123
Wilson, Woodrow, 219
Winston, Stephanie, 101
Witter, Dean, 42
Wooden, John, 41
Workman Page-A-Day Calendar,1987, 39
World Series, 29
World War I, 19, 121
Wright, Frank Lloyd, 215

Y

Yale University, 3

Z

Zalenik, Abraham, 237
Zappia, Dominick, 93
Ziege, W.W., 74
Ziglar, Zig, 77